Praise for *Letters to an Activist*

"There is a word that describes a person whose role is to fight evil daily: superhero. And every superhero has a special power with which to fight. But few superheroes have *every* power, which means they must learn how their particular specialty fits into the larger battle and how they can work together with other superheroes and their particular power. The world of activism is no different, and the letters and stories shared by Stephanie Clark are blueprints to be followed by anyone driven to be the change they want to see in the world. When we are tired, overwhelmed, or simply unsure of how or where to take the next step, these dispatches are direct, unvarnished, and authentic. Superhero activists, nonprofit leaders, and social entrepreneurs will find this book to be their agent of encouragement and their voice of faith and truth—intensely practical, clear-eyed truth."

—Doug Banks, editor, *Boston Business Journal*

"Here is a book that speaks to the heartache of a world broken by violence, hubris, and quick solutions. Stephanie has walked the long haul of providing space and healing for trafficked women. Daily she gets advice from would-be activists about how to do her job. Candid about both her frustration and her hope, she is a trustworthy guide for those who are seeking to be the change they want to see in the world. This is a compelling must-read for those who want to engage and not just pontificate about what is broken."

—Adele Calhoun, pastor and author

"Stephanie is calling us to get out of our own way, roll up our sleeves, and get our hands dirty by serving others in need. It's human nature to see a social injustice and want to fix it, but that isn't always the answer. The real, lasting social change begins when we humbly show up and do the work that's needed behind the scenes. Even when it's not an Instagram or Facebook worthy post."

—Jasmine Grace, founder and director,
Bags of Hope Ministries and author of
The Diary of Jasmine Grace: Trafficked. Recovered. Redeemed.

It's rare to find a book about activism or social justice that is both encouraging and realistic, hopeful and blunt, inspirational and grounded. *Letters to an Activist* is all these and humble too. I so appreciated the tone Stephanie took throughout the book, coming alongside the reader to share, to commiserate, to challenge, and to encourage. A reader will come away from this book with an understanding of the great need for activism because of profound evil and injustice, a sense of their own limitations and weak points, and a clear way forward in hope and faith and partnership with other activists. I recommend this book to anyone already invested in the work of justice and anyone who has an inkling they *should* be involved.

— Barnabas Piper, author and podcaster

"We are thirsty to discover hope in our pursuit of justice and *Letters to an Activist* offers us a beautiful cool cup of water to sate us on our way. Stephanie, in first person, thoughtful letters, shares her coming to consciousness as an activist as a guide for the true hero in the story, the reader. You will be inspired and filled with new ideas as you read each letter. This world needs more activists, and Stephanie is about the business of helping grow them in the wild fields of everyday life. Thank you, Stephanie, for your voice and commitment.

— Becca Stevens, leader, speaker and author

LETTERS
TO AN
ACTIVIST

Discovering Hope in the
Pursuit of Social Change

STEPHANIE CLARK

WESTBOW
P R E S S®
A DIVISION OF THOMAS NELSON
& ZONDERVAN

Scripture quotations marked NIV are taken from The Holy Bible, New International Version®, NIV® Copyright © 1973, 1978, 1984, 2011 by Biblica, Inc.® Used by permission. All rights reserved worldwide.

Scripture quotations marked ESV taken from The Holy Bible, English Standard Version® (ESV®), Copyright © 2001 by Crossway, a publishing ministry of Good News Publishers. All rights reserved.

This book is a work of non-fiction. Unless otherwise noted, the author and the publisher make no explicit guarantees as to the accuracy of the information contained in this book and in some cases, names of people and places have been altered to protect their privacy.

WestBow Press books may be ordered through booksellers or by contacting:

WestBow Press
A Division of Thomas Nelson & Zondervan
1663 Liberty Drive
Bloomington, IN 47403
www.westbowpress.com
1 (866) 928-1240

Because of the dynamic nature of the Internet, any web addresses or links contained in this book may have changed since publication and may no longer be valid. The views expressed in this work are solely those of the author and do not necessarily reflect the views of the publisher, and the publisher hereby disclaims any responsibility for them.

Any people depicted in stock imagery provided by Getty Images are models, and such images are being used for illustrative purposes only. Certain stock imagery © Getty Images.

ISBN: 978-1-9736-5557-2 (sc)
ISBN: 978-1-9736-5559-6 (hc)
ISBN: 978-1-9736-5558-9 (e)

Library of Congress Control Number: 2019902866

Print information available on the last page.

WestBow Press rev. date: 3/12/2019

Dedicated to
Mathia and Nevaeh

"If you read history you will find that the Christians who did most for the present world were just those who thought most of the next... It is since Christians have largely ceased to think of the other world that they have become so ineffective in this. Aim at Heaven and you will get earth 'thrown in': aim at earth and you will get neither."

—*Mere Christianity* by C. S. Lewis

Contents

Acknowledgments

This project began over a cup of coffee with the incredible Dr. Carter Crockett. We sat there discussing the women of Amirah and how God was working to bring about healing in a way we had never imagined possible. Carter casually said, "If you ever write a book, you should write letters to activists." I laughed and tried to act humble, but the idea struck a chord in me. Carter, this book would never have happened if you did not plant the seed of inspiration.

Along the way, there were several who came alongside me, encouraging me, challenging me, and helping me to finish the manuscript. Allison, thank you for affirming that this was a needed book. Mary, thank you for holding my feet to the fire. Heather, thank you for letting me vent and procrastinate. Nancy, thank you for being you, for reading through this in the first place, and for guiding me to finish it.

To Dawne and Katie, you are beyond inspiring to me. Thank you for always being there when I need you. You are the best sisters a girl could ever have.

To my husband, Dave, thank you for always believing in me, even when I don't. Thank you for your unbelievable support. Thank you for being a sounding board and for loving me through this process. To my girls, this book is dedicated to you. You saw mom in a whole new light through this process. Thank you for being my cheerleaders. I love you three more than you will ever know.

Introduction

I looked out at the audience and felt a sickness in my stomach. I had crossed a line; I could feel the tension on their faces. I had gone too dark too soon, and they were in shock about the evil they had just heard. I quickly needed to switch gears, so I grabbed a handful of candy that I happened to have up on the podium and said, "So... who could use a piece of chocolate?" Laughter cleared the air with a collective sigh. I said a quick prayer of gratitude and lightened the mood, reminding people that even amid great darkness, we can always find hope, because darkness is exactly where God wants us to shine a light.

I have shared this message time and again: shine light into darkness. When we do this, hope builds and rises up where there was none before. I have been amazed at the opportunities in my life to share this message, and the people I have been able to meet along the way. I have stood on the same stage as Becca Stevens, a woman I deeply admire and aspire to be. She has built an empire of social justice at Thistle Farms. I have sat in the room with Nobel Peace Prize winner Kailash Satyarthi, who at the time had physically freed over seventy thousand children from trafficking in India. His words still resound in my ears. I have the opportunity to train FBI agents, Department of Children and Families workers, and hospital social workers. I have shared at the Massachusetts State House and the United

Nations. Each time I share this message: even when this work feels overwhelming, we can have hope because of what we see happening when we provide someone with the opportunity to find freedom.

I am beyond grateful for the opportunities that have come my way. If someone had told me that this was going to be my life, I don't think I would have believed it. That is what typically happens in hindsight though—we sit back amazed at the journey that God has taken us on. There have been so many lessons that I have learned throughout the years of activism in my life. This book came about because I was challenged to share what I know.

I've always enjoyed correspondence. In fact, most of my days are filled with correspondence in one way or another. Emails and phone calls fill my time. When it came to writing out the lessons I have learned through my years of experience, it became natural for this book to be a correspondence through letter format. The questions being asked are real questions I have been asked throughout the years. I'm sure that there are plenty more out there that I don't address in this book, but I hope that these will help to guide you as you begin to pursue your dreams and passions.

My greatest hope is that this book will light a fire inside of you. If you are questioning whether to become an activist, I hope that this book will help you find your answer. If you are in the field already, I hope that it will offer you encouragement and give you new ways to sustain and move forward. As you will soon find out, I hope for many things. I have found it is the best way to live my life.

With hope, Stephanie

ONE

Be the Change

How do you get started with changing the world?
—ACTIVIST

Dear Activist:

During my first year of college in Chicago, I served in a soup kitchen every Sunday night for a semester. Each Sunday afternoon, three other students and I took the Red Line from Chicago Avenue all the way out to an area of Howard Street known as the Jungle.

Once we arrived, we helped to serve a meal that had been lovingly prepared by one of the kitchen's hardworking staff members. I remember one guy managed to transform the most unappealing can of peaches into a cobbler that belonged on a kitchen window somewhere in Georgia. He was a chef magician who turned ingredients that would be considered rubbish by most culinary standards into meals fit for kings.

Every Sunday, I scooped vegetables and potatoes onto plates and handed them off to the men who had walked in off the street. I was greeted with smiles and sometimes with inappropriate comments about my rear end but smiled back nonetheless. I knew that the circumstances of their day were far worse than those of my own.

Some of the men walked through the line with their heads down in a posture of shame. Some men I began to know by name because I saw them each week. Some men smiled and laughed and appeared to be having a great time. Some men cursed, and some spoke to voices they heard in the corner. Every single man had his own story, his own journey, but for now, they all found themselves in the same spot: needing a free meal and a warm place to lay their heads.

After the meal, we cleared the dishes and pushed the tables and chairs to the corners of the room, and the men grabbed mattress after mattress. Some had their own blankets; some had bags they pulled over themselves for added warmth. They settled in for the night, and my fellow students and I walked back out into the cold Chicago darkness to catch the L back to our dorm rooms.

After the first couple of weeks of feeling elated to be serving and helping, we grew in our cynicism—as many who have privilege tend to do. We wondered how much we were actually helping these men. Some men had been coming to this same soup kitchen every Sunday night for the past decade. We understood a meal and a place to sleep are great ways to meet immediate needs, but what we were doing wasn't solving the systemic problem. There were no counseling services, no job training, and no showers. What were a meal and a bed really going to do to combat a problem that was far bigger than the need for a place to sleep and some food to eat?

Week in and week out, the men shuffled in, said something wildly inappropriate to my face, and shoveled food into their empty bellies. They grabbed a mattress and shut the voices out. Food and a bed: that was why they were here. There was a sense of ritual to their movements; they had been here before and knew their part. But I couldn't see mine.

The four of us felt helpless. We felt more could be done. And as the semester wore on, we took it upon ourselves to lay out our solutions to the vast homeless epidemic that plagued Chicago. All we needed was for organizations to stop providing meals and putting out mattresses, which was the mission of this particular soup kitchen, and do exactly what we had cleverly and thoughtfully devised during the space of our forty-minute ride each week on the Red Line.

Hubris is the word that now comes to mind: excessive pride and self-confidence. I think back on those nights and feel so much guilt for my unbelievable hubris. The thing is I wasn't being asked by the soup kitchen to solve the problems of each of these men. I wasn't being asked by the mayor of Chicago for a better plan to tackle the long-standing issue of homelessness.

I was being asked to show up on time each week. To help get things ready in the kitchen. To make sure I didn't make a mess as I scooped food onto plates. To smile and be polite, even if the men there—because of the circumstances of their lives—were not exactly polite to me. I was there to wipe down tables and shove them into a corner. I was being asked to do this—and show up the next week to do it again.

It was Mahatma Gandhi who famously said, "You must be the change you wish to see in the world." This eloquent, powerful sentence has been quoted more than any other in the world of activism, but I often wonder if the people who quote it the most have actually lived it out.

As activists, we have what most people consider wild and crazy dreams. We believe that the world can be redeemed, that broken systems can really be fixed, and that people of opposing views can come together to solve the world's biggest problems.

The reality is that activists tend to live in these dreams rather than doing the work that has to be done. We think long and hard about the issue, we get increasingly upset about the issue, and we go so far as to devise elaborate systems in Excel spreadsheets to fix the issue, but we often bypass the part where we actually *become* the change in order to effectively address the issue. Why? Because it is easier, when we are heartbroken and upset by an issue, to fire something off on social media than it is to actively work, volunteer, and become the hands-on change that the issue requires. It is incredibly easy to get worked up and rant, but it is unfathomably hard to lay one's ego down and dedicate one's life to the work that already exists.

This means rolling up our sleeves, investing real time with those who are in the trenches of the movement (whatever movement you seek to join), and acknowledging that those people are a part of the larger system there to tackle the great problem that shouts at your heart and drives the passion inside you to action. That is the key: recognizing the cogwheel at work.

I am a small part in the movement of anti-trafficking. On a global scale, the impact that I have can be likened to a drip of water filling up the expanse of Lake Michigan. As of 2016, the human trafficking system profits $150 billion every year worldwide. That number is unfathomable. And the reality is that the work I do alone will never be able to decrease that number.

However, I am a part of a system and movement, and I have my place.

First, I am in a specific location within the world, within the United States, and even within the state of Massachusetts. Second, I am active in one part of the cogwheel of antitrafficking. I provide aftercare. I don't draft laws. I don't make arrests. I don't stop johns in their tracks. I raise awareness, but the awareness I raise is tailored to the trauma-recovery needs of the women who are getting out of the exploitation cycle. Third, I am in the world of aftercare, particularly caring for women who were sexually exploited and are now over the age of eighteen.

With all of this in mind, here is what I experience every week: I receive emails and phone calls and have conversations with people who suggest that I should be helping to stop johns from being able to purchase sex. If we can stop the demand for sex being purchased, they tell me, then the whole problem will go away. I am told also that I should open up beds to people who were labor trafficked, because labor trafficking is also a huge problem.

Every time I share about the women we serve, somebody with good intentions reminds me that boys and men are trafficked too and asks what I am doing about those victims. I am asked what I have done to help push through stronger laws within our state. I am asked why I do not get any funding from the government, as if the grants that are out there will somehow cover our massive expenses. This includes the salaries that need to be paid and the mortgage due every month. But they don't. Government grants are intended to cover special projects and require more work for an already overworked staff.

Each week, I am presented with solutions. I have been offered more used clothes than I care to mention. I have had well-meaning people who want to come and teach these extremely traumatized women yoga, people who want to come and have a Bible study with them, people who want to teach them how to dance, people who want to come and cook them a meal—but it can only be on Valentine's Day and the volunteers can only be there for two hours.

While every email, phone call, and face-to-face meeting is meant to offer a solution, it instead can create more work. The kicker is that when I respond to each of them with a polite rundown of the actual immediate needs we have, such as paying bills and needing people to invest at least four hours each month to be present in the home and to drive one or more women to appointments, I often get the response, "Well, I'm not sure that I would be able to do that. Let me know if you need anything else."

I don't.

The soup kitchen of my college days didn't need my ideas on how to solve the systemic problem of chronic homelessness. Their services were a part of the cogwheel at work. They were doing the active part of providing for a felt need: giving space for the night and allowing someone to feel warm, fed, and safe. They were a part of the journey of breaking free. There were others in the work to take care of the counseling needs, the need for job training, the need for financial mentoring. They were doing their part, and I missed out on seeing that because of hubris.

I was not being the change; I was trying to circumvent the change on my way to allegedly fixing the situation.

Activists, hear me: I understand the desire to want a quick fix, to be overwhelmed by the scale of the systems of suffering. The world is filled with suffering. It feels like there are more problems today than there were yesterday. Don't believe me? Just open up your news browser. It feels like, across the world and in our own backyards, there is more happening each day that causes suffering than is being done to provide peace, love, healing, and joy. But do we choose to be stunted by the overwhelming evil, or do we find the path we are to walk, head straight into the evil, and begin tirelessly to work against it?

I was once invited to be on a panel at Boston College to speak about the work of aftercare in the anti-trafficking movement. During the Q&A, a student wanted to know the most shocking thing I had heard in my field of work. I got the sense that he was simply fishing for a trafficking horror story, but even if that wasn't his intention, I wasn't biting. I looked at the young activists in the room and told them this: I believe that we live in a world where evil exists, and because of that we are capable of doing things to one another that would shock those who want to believe that everything is always bright, happy, and good. Then I let them know that because I believe in that, nothing shocks me. I have heard heartbreaking stories, but they do not shock me. It is evil, but I get to fight against that by providing a place where healing can happen. "I fight evil every day. It's fun," I said. "You should do it too."

I don't think it was the response that he or many in the room expected, but I hope that something sunk in there. There is real evil working to tear people down. But the role of the activist is to stand up against it and offer a better way—a way filled with hope, love, goodness, and freedom.

If those of us in the world in the business of fighting evil can do our part in the cogwheel, then the whole wheel turns, spinning and spinning and ultimately working to reverse what evil was done.

This is deep, hard work we are each called to do, but it starts with us becoming the change we want to see, not just offering up grandiose solutions for the problem.

All of the dreams we have will not come to fruition if we don't actually change our actions, thoughts, and selves.

In my life, this looks like providing a system and place where victims and survivors of sex trafficking can come and have a chance of finding hope and healing. However, this will not happen for them if I am not exercising in my own life a place of healing and a life of compassion.

The word for this is authentic.

My life has to be one of authentic healing in order for the women in my safe home to heal. My life has to be one where compassion overflows, where my heart is broken to action, not broken and paralyzed with inaction. If I do not practice these changes in my own life, why would I ever expect anyone else to do the same? Why would I expect the women who come into my care to be authentic in their own healing journey?

"Be the change you wish to see in the world," he said.

So how do you start? Most people are upset about the various injustices that occur around the world, but what is the one thing that keeps you awake at night? What is the thing that you see that you want to change? What is the evil that exists that you can no longer stand aside of—that you know deep in your heart you have to stand in the way of?

Discover that, then find out who is doing the work against it already (because they exist). Figure out their roles in the cogwheel. Do they work to prevent, to raise awareness, to be the actual hands that do the work, or maybe to make laws? This is a huge step in your discovery, because the last thing they need to hear is that they should be active in another part of the cogwheel. It is not why they exist; it is not their mission. They are supportive of the other parts of the wheel, but if they don't do their intended part, then no one will, and the wheel will never truly spin.

Then—and this is key—ask them what they need and then do that thing. Do the very thing they need. If it is volunteer hours, make yourself available. Be the change. If it is monetary donations, then sacrifice a coffee a week to start and give what you can to the cause. Be the change. If it is help with filing, then file papers. If it is stuffing envelopes, then stuff some envelopes. Be the change; don't be the burden.

Slowly, you will discover that you are becoming the person that is providing the very thing you wanted to see for so long. You see hope in the faces of those who experienced the very real evil. And all because you shut down your spreadsheets, you put aside your ego, you let go of the lofty ideas that you thought would be great and wonderful before you knew the issue from the inside out, and you simply learned what really helps, what really works, and you became that.

Authenticity over hubris—it changes lives.

With hope,
Stephanie

Shattering Mirrors

*I feel like I am supposed to be doing something different
with my life, but is it too late to make this change?*

—ACTIVIST

Dear Activist:

You are never too old or too young to be a part of something amazing. Activism is ageless. What it is not is being actionless.

I love Paul's exhortation to Timothy where he essentially lets the church know it is okay that this guy is young. "Don't let anyone look down on you because you are young, but set an example for the believers in speech, in conduct, in love, in faith and in purity."[1] Paul is writing this to Timothy, but it is a reminder to us all: just because someone is young doesn't mean that they aren't equipped by God to do the work.

When I began to think about writing a book, I felt a bit overwhelmed by the idea of this. One thought that kept creeping into my mind was that people would think I was too young, too inexperienced, too full of myself. In the grand scheme of things, they are right. I have not done very much. I don't have a Nobel Peace Prize. I have not run an organization for twenty-five-plus years. I am not retired and looking back. I probably don't have enough degrees behind my name. There is still so much I do not know. I admit that readily.

But these truths did not take away from what was being asked over and over again.

Someone was still coming to me asking to understand more about this work. People both young and old wanted to understand more, not just about sex trafficking, but about what it actually took to be an activist. Something inside was brewing up. I had something to answer, to write, to say. So, while I am quite aware that this may come off as hubris, I hope that you will see there is real humility here. I am aware of my age.

The women in the safe home of Amirah tend to be a bit ageist. When there is supposed to be one person in the home to make sure that everything remains safe, and that one person happens to be a young college student, they typically frown at this. Once, I had a woman come to me and say, "What on earth is this little girl going to do if my pimp comes to the door?"

It's a fair point. In that moment, the women of Amirah will have more experience than almost any college-age volunteer. But I pointed out to her that in the scenario she presented, she would have more experience than our staff who are older. Her distrust of the young volunteer was not because she was young, but because she was a human. She had not come to a point in her journey yet where she could trust other humans with her life.

Don't let others look down on you if you are young. Your calling, your desire to become an activist, is yours. Don't let anyone take that away from you. Go and learn, dive in with both feet, and do some amazing things to fight injustice in this world. I love having young people in the safe home at Amirah. Some of our best volunteers are young college students who desire to learn and grow. They don't come in thinking they know everything already; they just come in wanting to serve and love.

One of our greatest volunteers is a young woman named Taylor. She has been with us now for over three years, serving every single week for at least one shift a week. She was willing to learn about trauma; she was brave and courageous enough to be exposed to things she had never experienced before each week. She came ready and willing to do whatever was needed. We've watched her grow over the years. She shows up consistently and exudes a willingness to learn. The women have never felt like she was trying too hard. Instead, they saw her honesty, her humility, and her heart for them, and they welcomed her into their community. I am happy to say that she is now pursuing an MSW. I'm not sure that her time at Amirah can be the only thing to lay claim to her pursuing this, but I know that it helped her to find her path.

If we put a bar on how old you needed to be in order to volunteer with us, we would never have had the joy of getting to know Taylor. We would not have seen her grow and blossom. Being young should not deter you from getting involved. It is the perfect time to explore and grow in your experience. It is a time to learn and see what you really are called to be doing. It is a time to stretch yourself and develop a work ethic that pursues excellence in all things. Don't let anyone tell you that you are too young to begin in the world of activism. Go, get involved.

Likewise, don't let others look down on you because you are too old to get into the game. I remember a conversation I had with a woman when I was a pastor. She was in her early sixties and was pretty sad, bordering on becoming upset, because she felt like she had missed out on something God wanted her to do with her life.

As she spoke about what she felt like God had called her to do, she was convinced that this dream was meant for her thirty years ago. It was a big dream. It required a lot of work. It was a bigger vision than she felt like she could do at this time in her life. I sat there a bit heartbroken for her because she was unable to see and realize that God still wanted her to do what He had put on her heart now. It was so clear that He was taking all of her life experience and everything she had done, building it up to this point in her life. He wasn't asking her to go back in time; He was nudging her that He still had some incredible work for her to do now. The dream felt to her that it required young blood, but what it needed was someone experienced to lead it.

I think Paul's point to Timothy should go both ways. Don't let anyone look down on you or dismiss you because you are too young *or* too old. You might not have as much energy when you are older as when you were in your twenties, but you will have more wisdom.

One of my favorite volunteers at Amirah is an older woman named Anne. I hope that I am allowed to say that: yes, I do have favorites! When I first met Anne, who I affectionately refer to as "Grandma Anne," I thought there was no way this woman was going to be able to cut it. She looked too old, too kind, too easy to push around. I thought the survivors would dismiss her immediately and that she would never volunteer again because they said a crude joke to her.

But, thankfully, I was wrong. Anne showed up and did exactly what we asked all volunteers to do: be present. She didn't treat the women like children she was babysitting. She didn't ask them inappropriate questions about their past. She didn't watch them like fish in a fishbowl. She just came, served quietly, and was present for them, tending to their needs. When a woman had an appointment, she would drive her. If we needed something picked up at the store, she would run the errand. If a woman had a two-hour doctor's visit, Anne would sit there patiently with her.

Anne did what we asked every volunteer to do. She showed up for the women consistently. She loved them without forcing anything on them. She didn't come in with expectations about what she could do with them, all of the things she could teach them, or about how her time with them was supposed to be. She came in with humility and love, allowing these women to feel like someone cared for them.

Pretty soon, I watched as Anne become someone that was important to the survivors. Something happens when they see a stranger come in and give her time week after week. Their walls of defense and protection begin to break down. As Anne showed up, they saw that she cared for them. She didn't come into the home asking to teach them something or acting like she knew more than them. She just came in and loved them.

When the winter came, I walked into the safe home to find Anne serving her normal weekly morning shift. She was in our project room teaching a woman how to make a quilt. Here was this amazing grandma and a woman who had lived most of her life on the streets sitting down making a beautiful quilt together. I could hardly believe my eyes.

When the winter began to thaw into spring, Anne was out in the garden with two women who wanted to learn from her how to garden.

We hear often from people that they want to come into the safe home and teach the women something. It could be yoga, it might be how to cook, it might be how to do their makeup for job interviews. While these requests are good, it doesn't work like that when you are working with attachment disorders, significant trust issues, and trauma. These women need to get to know you. They need a relationship. They need to see that you are willing to invest in them, and then maybe, if they actually like your personality, you might be able to sit down with them and do something together, if it is something that she really does want to learn. We always ask these people to just come and volunteer. Come and be a part of their lives. Activate something inside of you that desires to see change: be the change in your own life, before you go and change another's life.

Anne did not shy away from getting involved in a cause that she was passionate about because she would have been deemed as "too old." She did not come into the space thinking that she knew everything already. Instead, she came in, she learned, she grew, and she gave wholeheartedly. Because of that, she is one of my absolute favorite volunteers.

The reality is that the world of activism is not about you. It is never about how old or young you are. It is not about all of the amazing things you will do. It is about someone else. For me, this world is about giving time and space to a survivor to watch her become the woman that God created her to be and leave behind the slave she was forced to be.

If you are afraid to get involved because you are too young or too old, I beg you to reconsider. Take a look in the mirror and shatter the doubts that plague you. There is so much that needs to be done and so much that you can offer. Injustice will always spin its ugly wheel, but that wheel gets slower each time someone steps into this world of activism to fight against it.

What is stopping you from taking that next step? Hopefully it is not your reflection in the mirror.

The beautiful thing that happens when you change your life is that your change impacts another's life. I am often reminded that the Amirah home would not exist if I had not taken the next step in my journey. I had serious doubts about my capabilities. I wondered if I was experienced enough to do this work. I thought I was too young to be an executive director. I didn't know if people would respect me as their boss. I didn't know if the women in the home would believe in me or not.

At some point, though, if you are going to become an activist, you have to let your ego go. This world is not for the thin-skinned. Of course, there are people who think I am too young. I get labelled as inexperienced a lot of the time. The women will naturally distrust me from the moment they meet me. But none of this is about me. Activism is never about me, and it is not about you either.

You have a chance to bring pockets of heaven to this earth. Detach your ego and dive in. With hope,

Stephanie

THREE

Rest in Calling

How do you know you are called to do something?

—ACTIVIST

Dear Activist:

Calling is such a hot button word nowadays. There are articles, chapters, and even whole books devoted to helping people figure out "the calling" on their lives, particularly within Christian circles. I know that when I was nineteen years old, I felt this pressure to have my entire ministry life planned and plotted out; I had to have a clear calling into ministry, or I was going to be found out to be a fraud. While I am sure that most of that pressure was self-imposed, after talking with a few friends who experienced the same thing as well as hundreds of people now heading into ministry training, I have found this is a common pressure.

I would like to tell you to stop putting that pressure on yourself, but I know this is an uphill battle against a downward, hurricane-force wind. It can feel like the entire Christian world wants you to know your calling, to rely on that and be able to clearly define and spell it out in a catchy fifteen words or less. It doesn't help that there are emotionally charged worship songs that focus on this as well—I see you "Oceans."[2]

What is the big deal about a calling? We almost have to ask this, right? Is this a normal thing? Do people in the secular world have anything like this? I mean, we hear about career paths and career trajectories. There are five-year plans and the pursuit of doing something you would do even if you had $20 billion. So, is the Christian word for this a calling?

In a way, quite possibly. It might be that it is such a hot button word among us because the real world is attempting to provide people with opportunities to feel like they are doing something with their lives that they want to do. The reality is that no matter what job you are in, you will spend more waking hours in that job and with your coworkers than you will with your family.

The world has seen that and developed an entire culture now around workplace enjoyment because of this. There are so many huge corporations that have work perks to keep their employees happy. I'm thinking here of the Google campus where nap pods are known to provide creative space for employees. The large tech firms that have gyms housed on campus, or a ping-pong table where employees can let out stress. Workplace enjoyment, because you will spend most of your time here.

The Christian world in part has reacted to this and placed a huge emphasis on calling. But what is a calling? *Merriam-Webster* gives us definitions that calling is a strong inner impulse toward a particular course of action, especially when accompanied by conviction of divine influence; or the vocation or profession in which one customarily engages. I like that phrase—a conviction of divine influence—don't you? It's more than just this feeling about liking something. It goes deep into who you are.

I appreciate the verse in Ephesians where Paul lets us know we are God's workmanship created by Him for good works.[3] It is affirming that what I do in my life can and should be what God actually created me for. Not only was I created for this, I am called to do it. I might just be really good at what I do because this is the exact thing that God made for me. The same is true for you and your divine conviction.

It can be extremely strenuous as you are trying to figure out what this divine conviction is in your life. I have had so many conversations with young people who are attempting to find out what they should do, as well as older people who are rethinking their lives, that they almost become stunted in fear of taking a step forward.

Thoughts plague them, *What if I'm wrong? What if I make a mistake and end up doing something I was never supposed to do? What if I waste years of my life and thousands of dollars for a degree that isn't going to help me? What if I make this huge change and don't make enough money to live?*

I joke around with my board that they have an executive director who has a degree in biblical languages. Their ED can read and translate Greek! It's great for tattoos, not so much for holding the trauma of a survivor of sex trafficking. Was my degree a waste? Was the decade of my life leading up to this ministry all for naught? I sure hope not!

I learned how to study. Nothing taught me more about the need for hard study than my degree in biblical languages.

There are many things you can fake in life. If you are a good speaker, you can possibly wing a speech here and there and get away with it. However, you cannot fake being put on the spot by your Greek professor when he or she is asking you to translate in front of the entire class.

This time led me to learn how to be disciplined and diligent. There were so many nights when I just wanted to veg out and chill with my friends. It didn't help that I met my future husband as well during these years. I would much rather have hung out with him, talking about anything and nothing at all, than to sit and memorize Greek vocabulary words. But discipline and diligence in my time became the necessity. If I didn't have this, I wouldn't be able to study and focus on the task at hand.

It made me into a critical thinker. I learned it was okay to ask questions, and then I learned how to ask the right questions. I processed information and began to put puzzle pieces together. I was asked to find solutions and learned how to deal with stress.

This is true for many people, though, who have the experience of higher education. Those years are fruitful times of learning discipline. How does this apply to it being a part of your calling? Because calling is not in a silo. God utilizes everything that happens in our lives to shape us toward the calling He is giving to us.

I am so grateful for these gifts in my life. In the decade leading up to going into full-time ministry, I had the gift of exploration. I had years of growing pains. I learned the harsh truth that there were many times when I needed to keep my mouth shut and listen. I am often quite aware that if I were doing what I do now when I was twenty-one, this would have been a complete failure from the start. I would have offended and hurt more than I would have been able to help and offer hope.

I learned how to love and give sacrificially during these growing years. There are things that get discussed on a theoretical level in classroom spaces that really never hit home until you are in the trenches experiencing it. You can translate and study the Gospel of John, but you won't fully understand this gospel until you see the call to live out the radical commands of Jesus in it. I realized that loving others was hard, but that it was the thing that was needed the most. Not only did I learn how to give that kind of love to others and still hold on to the boundaries I need to have rest in my life, I learned about what makes me tick, what I am truly passionate about, and ultimately, I learned about what I am called to do.

It was intensely practical.

After I became a pastor, in one of the first weeks on the job, I sat with a woman who had miscarried her child. I didn't know she wanted to talk to me about this; she just unloaded the sad news over coffee. She wasn't asking for answers, she was asking to be heard, to be loved. If I had sat across from her as my twenty-one-year-old self, I would have been quick to give her answers. But a decade of life lessons and the personal experience of my own miscarriage had me sitting there in silence—offering her an ear and tears of sadness.

Calling might be a moment in time for some people, a divine word or vision or audible affirmation—"Go and be a missionary in this small village in West Africa." But for most of us, it is a journey and process. Some of us recognize this journey along the way, but there are others who see their calling in hindsight as they look back at their lives. It is what shapes you and forms you. For me, the affirmations came along the way. It was as if God was shaping me and molding me each day as I grew to become this; once I was ready, the calling on my life to do this was so evident that there wasn't a doubt in my mind when I made the transition to the work of aftercare for survivors of sex trafficking.

My hope and prayer for you is that you would realize that calling does not have to be this scary, impossible thing, but that it actually is a beautiful, organic part of the journey of faith that God has for you.

What are the markers you have seen in your life where you have felt affirmed? Have you recognized that feeling when you are doing something where you feel this complete wholeness about who you are? Have you ever felt that or anything resembling that? If so, go after that—follow the rabbit trail and discover what God has for you. A quick pause, though, that while you do this, you remember the beautiful verse from the psalms where the songwriter says, "I shall walk in a wide place…"[4] What a beautiful image to put with the will of God. It is not a needle in a haystack, but a wide place to walk in your journey of faith. So don't sit back passively waiting for the needle to present itself. Go take a walk in the wide place and watch God unfold His big, beautiful plan for your life.

Now, a word of caution, my dear activist: please do not mistake your personal journey of healing for a true calling. I work with a heavily traumatized population. Whenever I have the opportunity to add employees, my initial reaction is dread. I dread having to comb through résumés and have first-round interviews with people who will tell me that they want to work with survivors of sex trafficking because they themselves were abused as a kid, and they want to help others heal the same way they were healed. They can't wait to share their stories with the women and feel like it will help the women immediately be able to recover and heal.

This doesn't mean that I am against someone working with us that has gone through abuse; it is that I dread hearing this as the first reason why they want to work with this population. It becomes their identity—I was healed; therefore, I want to heal others. This might sound absurd and contradictory to what I have been writing here, but I promise you it is not meant to be. There is a fine line between being affirmed in your calling from God, where you utilize your experience from your past, and thinking that somehow your journey of healing is exactly what others need to hear in order for their healing to happen.

This is what I like to call the savior complex. It starts with the reason that you got into this job was because you "want to give back" and ends with you burning yourself out because you were not ready to hold the trauma of someone else. When their healing didn't happen the way yours did, and they chose a path of destruction rather than a hard day of trauma-recovery work, you are crushed. Do not mistake your healing from trauma with a calling from God. This is worrisome at best and dangerously destructive at worst—for you and those you serve.

Your healing is just that, *your* healing. It is a part of your journey. It is an incredible gift from God and can most definitely be used to guide and shape you. But healing is not a calling, it is a gift. Calling is the undeniable truth that sits before you each day that this work you are setting out to do was exactly why God created you. You are His workmanship, and He created you to carry out some good, amazing works.

With hope,
Stephanie

FOUR

Why People Will Never Be as Passionate as You

How do you handle it when people do
not want to support what you do?

—ACTIVIST

Dear Activist:

I have spent the better part of a decade reluctant to tell people my career. Before I was the executive director for Amirah, I was an associate pastor. When I was introduced to strangers, nothing killed the conversation faster than when they found out I was one of those weirdo pastors who would probably try to convert them. Especially in Massachusetts, where most people are agnostic and unchurched, they would almost run away from me. I distinctly remember one woman saying to me, "A pastor? Huh! I didn't know people went to church anymore." Yeah, that was a great conversation that lasted a total of 2.5 seconds.

It is not much better now when I tell them what I do. Most people feign some sort of shocked face. "What? Sex trafficking? How horrible! You are a saint." And then they don't want to discuss this horrible, stressful, disgusting topic anymore, letting me know they simply must go say hi to someone they just saw. I don't blame them. It is an unpleasant topic and a very hard one for people to wrap their minds around.

I often talk about busting down the myths and spend most of my days doing this with the general population. Yes, sex trafficking exists right here in America. Yes, there are women, boys, and girls all being trafficked. Yes, it is American women being trafficked, not just foreign nationals being trafficked here—as if that should matter.

Nine times out of ten, I watch as the roller coaster of emotions plays out before me. First, there is the shock that this is happening. Some sort of exclamation about how they can't believe it or are so disgusted by this! Second, there is the blame placing. Blaming the traffickers, blaming the buyers, blaming the politicians who don't do anything about this, blaming whichever president is sitting or was sitting that they simply didn't like, blaming the police who don't do enough to stop this. There is always a lot of blame to go around. Third, it is the solutions that only they can think of. They offer everything under the sun from their used clothes to some essential oil that helped them with their anxiety. While this is endearing, it isn't helpful (see my first letter). They promise, though, to be passionate about this, to tell their friends, to get involved, and most importantly, to send a check to support us.

Lastly, they simply move on. The check never comes. They don't get involved. They don't even tell their friends. They move on because they were overwhelmed.

This happens again and again. It is a vicious cycle.

A young woman who worked for me was incredibly passionate about working with victims of sex trafficking. She was a strong advocate in public for this. She chimed in on social media about every story in the news. She let everyone know how much she cared. The problem was that she was constantly offended by her friends and family who didn't care about this issue as much as she did. It seemed like a no-brainer to her. This was evil at its worst, and if you are a human being and have a heart, you should fight against this evil. But they didn't.

I remember when I was a kid and sat at home all summer long. I was a fan of watching all the daytime television I could while my parents worked. Without fail, every morning at 11:33, a commercial came on featuring Sarah MacLachlan. Yes, this was pre-DVR, fast-forwarding capabilities, so I had to watch the commercials. The commercial flashed up pictures of dogs and puppies who had been abused and needed help. In the background, her heart-tugging song "I Will Remember You" was playing softly.

At the end, she sat there with a rescue dog on her lap, pleading and asking that you remember these dogs and send some money today to support the work of this organization.

This commercial had everything: horrible pictures that made you feel terrible, cute pictures of dogs that you wanted to help, and Sarah MacLachlan—my generation's voice of an angel. But I never helped the dogs. Now, you could argue I was a kid and didn't have any money or a credit card, so I really couldn't, but I never talked to my parents about this issue. I simply let the problem pass over me and moved on with *The Price is Right.*

No amount of cute dog pictures was going to move me to action, mostly because I was allergic to dogs. But I'm sure those commercials did tug on the hearts of others and they sent along support.

Not everyone will be as passionate as you about your cause. We are not built to have that much capacity for empathy and compassion.

I am never more reminded of this truth than in January, which in America is the National Anti-Trafficking Month or Human Trafficking Awareness Month, or in July when it is World Awareness of Trafficking in Persons Day. People walk around with red X's on their hands in the hope that someone will ask them about the X's.

While I'm sure these days are important, part of me feels overwhelmed by them. There are so many days singled out now for various injustices. There are marches in every major city, seemingly on a weekly basis. Everyone has some fund-raiser they support on social media. They donate their birthdays to support causes, they do walks, they bike one hundred miles. People are passionate, but does that mean they have to be passionate about your cause?

I have become almost apologetic now when I introduce myself to people. Instead of telling them off the bat what I do, I let them know I run a nonprofit. Sometimes they ask which one, and I let them know what we do and who we work with, and then I give them a moment to either engage or not. If they don't, I'm ready to reciprocate and talk with them about their work or family. Not everything has to be about me and my cause.

This may sound like a nightmare to the development committee on Amirah's board, but I can assure you it is purposeful and has paid off in spades in the end.

I want to cultivate relationships. I want to know people

and have them know me. I want them to know what brings me the greatest joy in my life. I want them to see my passion and drive, rather than have it rammed down their throats in some elevator pitch. That's not to say I don't have an elevator pitch; I can bring you to your knees in a matter of fifteen seconds like the best of champs. But we have to stop expecting our cause will be everyone's cause.

There is just simply too much happening in this world. The list of injustices grows every year. Evil gets more creative and nuanced. More money is required as government funding resources dry up. More governments are shown to be corrupt, and thus the vicious cycle starts again in some places.

The truth is, though, that if you cannot stop your instant rage at the masses who are not as enraged as you are because of the injustice that has your heart, you have some work to do, not the masses.

It's time to take a look inward and begin to ask some questions. Why am I so passionate about this issue? What has happened in my life to cause this particular injustice to strike a chord with me? What am I doing with my time, talent, and resources to make sure I am bringing justice where there is injustice?

As you reflect on those answers, it will become easier to see that this is a very deep, personal thing for you. At least, I hope it is. I would hate to give my life to something that isn't. I find that when something is personal, it is easier to see that it shouldn't be for everyone. It's assuming things of others, and we all know what that does to you.

If I am passionate about an issue, then I need to pursue it with all of my heart, mind, soul, and strength. There is nothing in my life that brings me greater joy than watching a woman who was exploited find her journey of liberation in an Amirah safe home. But I can't expect that joy to be yours. Sarah MacLachlan can't expect her passion for puppies to be mine either. Again, I'm allergic, so it's almost a nonstarter. But I bet in a few years, when my youngest daughter is holding down a steady job and is ready to start giving back to others, she may very well find the local shelter and devote some time and resources to it. She loves dogs, and they love her. At times, I wonder if she loves our neighbor's dog more than me, but she assures me she does not. However, it is the dog's picture that is hanging up next to her desk, not mine. But I digress.

Passion must be connected to all of this. We live in a world where evil is more and more creative every year. No human being has enough capacity, strength, or emotional support to be passionate about every issue. It simply is impossible. If we had that kind of strength, then we would be Jesus. Even then, it was His strength specifically for taking on all of the evil and injustice and sin of the world that was what led Him to the cross. That is where that kind of weight is borne.

I am not Jesus. You are not Jesus. We cannot expect others to be either. So just because no one responds to your very impassioned plea on whatever social media platform you use about the boldest news headline on the latest atrocity, it does not mean this is not something you should be working against. It just means it is something *you* should be working against, not your neighbor. Don't get me wrong, evil is wrong all of the time, and we should all know that and be abhorred by it. But we all don't have to fight all of it all at the same time.

You are His workmanship created for His good works, remember? He has a specific job for you, He has one for me, and He has one for your friends as well. Don't get that mixed up. Do your job. Don't expect others to do it for you or to join you.

With hope, Stephanie

FIVE

When Faith Meets Action

How can you deal with such pain
and trauma all of the time?

—ACTIVIST

Dear Activist:

I remember the day the safe home of Amirah opened. My staff and I were a bit overwhelmed—we really had no idea what we were getting ourselves into. All we knew was that we needed to love these women and take it a day at a time.

The day I met our first survivor, Jessie, I attempted to remain as calm as possible in front of her. I knew she was overwhelmed and wanted to run, so I didn't want to show her how scared I was. I spent most of the car ride home that night crying. I didn't know her story yet, but I knew she had been through torment to get into our home. She might have been a stranger to me sitting there on the couch with bright red hair and sunglasses on to hide her eyes, but in the car ride home it hit me that she was my sister and love started to flood my heart.

As the days turned into weeks and we saw more women come into the safe home, I began to watch John 1:5 come to life right before my eyes.

"The light shines in the darkness, and the darkness has not overcome it."[5]

I will never fully understand the evil and darkness these women have been through. I hold their stories in my heart, but I do not understand them. But I was not asked to understand or somehow justify these stories, placating their experience and lives. Instead, I am asked to shine light into the darkness they have lived.

This sounds mystical, I know, but let's put away our academia caps for a moment and step into the world where we live and move and have our being, shall we?

Psalm 139 is this beautiful poem about the connection between God and everything that we are. In it, the psalmist writes about how God knows his days, how God is always with him. "Where can I go from your presence?" As if there is an answer to that. Because even if the psalmist is in darkness, God is there. "Even the darkness is not dark to you; the night is bright as the day, for darkness is as light with you."[6]

Gustavo Gutierrez writes that "the Lord is not intimidated by the darkness. His light grows stronger in the shadows."[7]

We can choose to be overwhelmed by evil and stuck in a constant cycle of despair, or we can walk into the darkest part of that evil and believe that Jesus will be with us there.

Here is how I have learned to walk into the darkness.

One time, I was at a conference and a preacher was talking about how he prepared for the day each morning. He opened up the Bible and read out Ephesians 6, the armor of God passage. He then described his morning where he quite literally went through the motions as he stepped out of his bed and put on the various armor pieces as he prepared himself for his day.

Let me first say, if that is you and your daily morning routine, then that is awesome. I don't do that, though. It is not that I believe the armor of God is unreal or anything like that; quite the contrary. I very much believe in everything God has given us to equip us to live this life here on this fallen earth.

I just want to prepare you that as I discuss what I have learned about how to walk into darkness each day, I really am not going to be as practical as putting on the belt of truth each morning.

The truth is I am probably one of the most laid-back darkness walkers that you will meet. When I was a pastor, I met with several people on an individual basis for pastoral counseling. There were a handful of people who were a bit fanatical about the power of Satan. When I shared this with a fellow pastor, he joked that it seemed like they were seeing demons under every rock. It certainly felt that way.

I remember sitting with one woman in particular who was convinced that a dark power was in her home. I prayed with her, prayed throughout the home, anointed it with oil, and assured her that He who is in her is stronger than anything in this world. I don't think she believed me though, because I didn't call down fire and brimstone on whatever was in her home. I just simply spoke the name of Jesus and believed He would indeed do what He promised to do.

I think this certainty came about because early on in my journey of faith I read C. S. Lewis's *Screwtape Letters*. Satan is not the nemesis of God; he isn't even on the same playing field. He is a fallen angel, not a fallen god. And if you are a believer in Jesus and everything He has done for you, then the promise that the Holy Spirit dwells inside you is quite an amazing one. God dwells in you. Why should we worry about a fallen angel?

With this in mind, this is how I start off my day: Reminding myself of this amazing promise and attuning my spirit with the Spirit, shedding off the academia for a moment, and stepping into the reality of what living with the Holy Spirit indwelling a person can mean. Most mornings, I start my day by just sitting in silence and waiting. I'm reminded that God comes to us in the sound of sheer silence, not in the fire, the wind, a shattering earthquake.[8]

It can be very scary to start your day in silence. Our minds will often play tricks on us. Mine wants to start working right away. It is thinking of my to-do lists and running through the million things I need to get done before 9:00 a.m. It often does begin to run through my lists, but then I sit a little while longer and work to center myself toward God.

The Bible often talks about where we fix our eyes (Hebrews, Psalms), so I literally fix my eyes on this window in my home that looks outside to the trees and the beautiful sunrise, and then I sit silently and wait to hear from God.

There is no audible voice that comes, but rather this immense peace—a peace that goes far past anything I can understand and centers me. It is the reminder that He is with me. The reminder that I am not alone. The reminder that He can move mountains, He can guide me, He can protect me. He is a rock, a fortress, a shield. Not only that, but He is *my* rock, *my* fortress, *my* shield.

And from there, I start my day. There are very few things that will rattle my cage after spending some time in silence listening for God.

The next thing I do is begin to pray without ceasing. Yes, that little phrase from Paul that drives everyone nuts. What on earth does the apostle mean by praying without ceasing? Am I supposed to talk incessantly in my head or out loud to God all day every day? Wouldn't I look insane? Couldn't that possibly lead me to insanity?

I find that praying without ceasing does not mean a state of constant chatter. Prayer is a conversation where two are conversing together, both speaking and listening. Most of the day, I am listening. I am asking God for wisdom on where He wants the light shined, how to shine it, when to shine it, and then I am waiting for that nudge to go ahead.

I've heard it described that every job that exists is solving problems in some way, shape, or form. So when you think about the job you want to do, you really just need to figure out what problems you want to spend your time solving.

As you grow into leadership, your capacity for solving problems only grows. I receive dozens of questions each day that require problem-solving skills. Most are aimed right at the darkness we are dealing with. I wish the questions were as simple as should we purchase romaine lettuce or iceberg, but they are not. It often involves stories of trauma, mental health disorders that are flaring up in response to trauma-recovery work, and the daily task of keeping a safe home actually safe and secure.

This is where that whole praying without ceasing really comes in handy. As I spend my day and moments talking to God and listening for Him, these problems at hand become a part of my prayer life. I don't just give answers to these problems willy-nilly. I pause and bring this matter into the constant prayer that is flowing between God and me. Nine times out of ten, I end up going ahead with my ever-wise gut and everything works out just fine. But every once in a while, what I want to do in my gut is not matching what the Spirit is telling me.

It's at these moments that I either choose to be obedient or stubbornly go with my way. Usually when I win, a disaster follows, and then we end up doing what the Spirit was nudging me about in the first place.

Pray without ceasing means your day is spent in constant communication, talking or listening to God. You become an incredible multitasker as you do this. Most people I encounter have no idea that I have a prayer life happening right then and there as we are talking. But this practice is exactly what helps as I walk into incredibly dark situations.

We often have women in our safe home dealing with past misdemeanors and felony charges while they are actively working on their trauma-recovery. While we will not be their jail to serve out time, we will go and vouch for a woman in court to show the judge that she is making progress toward starting a new life.

Kristine[9] had her last court date for a felony charge while she was in our home. Her hope was she would be able to show the judge she was working on changing her life and that he would drop the charge down to a misdemeanor and let her work on a payment plan to pay a fine, rather than getting kicked back to jail. However, the court and judge were back in her hometown where she had spent a good portion of her life in the cycle of exploitation and drug dealing. It was a full day's drive to get there, but we packed up my car and made the trek.

As we entered this town in Maine, I felt a deep darkness and sadness weigh on me. This town reminded me of Detroit when Detroit was at its worst. It was economically depressed. The people living in it were running on empty. The children were running meth labs from their homes. Most were dying on the streets because they simply could not get out of there. This was where this woman I loved so much had lived her life. Everything about who she was and how she became the hard woman I knew was because of this town and what it did to her.

This was darkness.

I spent the night in the local motel, knowing full well that I would be spending the night in a place where she had been trafficked. I didn't sleep that night. I did everything I could to scrub myself clean in the morning, but there was nothing that could remove this heaviness and feeling of complete dirt all over me.

I put worship music on in my car and let God's light begin to shine. I never felt abandoned by Him, but if you don't begin to remind yourself of His presence, you can forget He is there. The courthouse was filled with people who looked like Kristine when she showed up in our home. They were run-down and tired. They had put themselves together as best they could, but you could tell they were itching for their next fix. She knew most of their faces. Some looked at her in her suit and blouse, something she picked out especially for this trip, with a look of disdain. Almost as if Kristine was too good for them now.

I felt for her.

I watched as person after person was called up before the judge. For some he dealt out harsh penalties, for others he showed leniency. I couldn't read him, but I wondered if he thought that his career as a judge would be marked with dealing with addicts who stole cars because they were too high to know better.

The next thing I knew, it was her turn. I could feel her tension, her stress, her fear, but somehow, she walked confidently to the stand. It was like a stream of light walking through the darkness. She pled her case, and the judge asked if she had a witness. I came up to the stand and watched as light began to shine into the darkness. I was able to talk to the judge and let the others in the room hear how well Kristine was doing. How she was changing her life and showing that she desired to live a clean, sober life. She had a job and was excelling at it. She had a car and was paying her bills.

The judge looked at me inquisitively and said, "Boston is kind of far. How come you are all the way up here for her?"

And this is when light began to take over the whole room. I don't know why, but the first thing I said was, "Because I love her. I would do anything for her. She is worth it."

Her case had been heard, the judge was gracious and lenient, and she was free to go after we stopped off to pay a fine.

As I wrote earlier, I often tell young college students who are fishing for trauma stories that I fight evil each day, and it's fun. This is completely true. But, if I could, I would add to that statement. It gives me more joy and fulfillment than anything else in this world. Not only is fighting evil fun, it is the very thing that God is doing. Shine light into darkness—this is what He does. He grows stronger in the darkness shining His light. And since He lives in you, my dear activist, you grow stronger too.

With hope, Stephanie

SIX

Seeking Conflict

What are the greatest misconceptions
about being an activist?

—ACTIVIST

Dear Activist:

We were two weeks away from celebrating the graduation of
the first woman we welcomed into the home of Amirah, an
amazing woman named Jessie. We were all a bit emotional over
this graduation, as Jessie was our first for so many things, and
to see her ready to go out and be on her own was an amazing
triumph.

So, with two weeks to go, I received a forwarded email
from our program director, Heather. It came from one of our

volunteers who had experienced a rough evening. All of the women in the safe home were in a season where they were a bit on edge and their emotions were running high. We had done our best to prepare volunteers for the range of emotions they would see, but we knew they would need a little more hand-holding during this time.

This volunteer had experienced an incident while driving the women for appointments. Some minor disagreement among the women had escalated and voices were louder than our volunteer was used to. Since she was new to volunteering with us, this argument alarmed her, as it would most people. But she calmly reported everything that happened so that we could work with the women the following day. However, one phrase caught my eye in the email. She spoke about Jessie and let us know that she wasn't sure if this woman was ready to graduate based on what she saw the previous night. Then she closed with a passive-aggressive statement that she knew we had Jessie's best interest at heart.

It was then I realized that I had to speak more often about managing expectations. This wonderful volunteer had just started to volunteer with us recently. She had only known Jessie for maybe three interactions over the course of a couple of months. She had not seen the growth this trauma survivor had undergone. She was not there for the first few weeks when Jessie would suffer from night terrors. She did not get the silent treatment from her. She did not have to look at a woman who hid behind sunglasses and a hooded sweatshirt. The first time I attempted to talk with Jessie was a phone call. When she finally realized that she did not know who I was, she hung up on me. This volunteer never experienced these things. She never walked Jessie through months of panic attacks. She did not see the emotional growth through the months and years.

She only knew a trauma survivor who still had a bit of an edge to her and at times would let her emotions fly. I had the feeling this volunteer and quite a few other people were expecting victims of sex trafficking to go through the Amirah program and come out completely healed, acting like people in the world who had not gone through trauma. I had the sense they were expecting them to come out and be like them. The reality, though, is that these women are going to work through their program and learn some incredible coping skills. They are going to learn how to manage their emotions and respond to triggers. They will tackle their addiction and choose sobriety. They will hold down a job and show responsibility to their employers and themselves. They will discover the power of forgiveness and release the hold that the cycle of shame had on their lives.

They will do all of these things and remain their amazing selves. This means that they will have an edge to them. They won't trust easily. They will never really feel comfortable around squares.[10] They will rise to a challenge, especially when it is one of their own challenging them. I can't expect her to become me. I need to expect her to become the amazing woman that God created her to be.

I think that most activist leaders out there would agree with me no matter what field they are in that expectations are hard to meet. There are expectations from our donors on how we will spend their money. There are expectations from grant funders on how much return on investment they will see in the project they are funding. There are expectations from volunteers and interns that they will do a level of work that is typically reserved for paid staff. There are expectations from staff that they will have enough time in their day to get all of their work done. There are expectations from the public that our work will provide solutions and change on a scale that far exceeds our budget.

We deal with a lot of expectations in the work of activism.

One of the greatest challenges out there is the expectation that our work will result in complete freedom from conflict. Whatever problem or injustice you are working against, there is the expectation that your work will solve the problem. The injustice will go away.

I work in the field of anti-trafficking. When I started this work, the Global Slavery Index reported that the worldwide profit of all forms of human trafficked was $32 billion. Just three years after I started this work, that number had grown to $150 billion. If my expectation was that I was going to help this problem dissolve and go away, I would have been failing miserably at that.

The problem is with almost every injustice that we face, we have to deal with systemic problems that can reach back for hundreds, sometimes thousands of years. The harsh reality we must face as activists is that we will not stop the systemic problems completely in our work. We can be a part of the solution and make strides so that the next generation does not have to do the exact same work we do, but we will not be the final answer.

I think about the work of anti-trafficking and how much effort it takes. Slavery is not new to us. Treating human beings as commodities has been around since before Jesus walked the earth. I think if the abolitionists before us were to say they had solved the problem of slavery and fixed the injustice completely, then we would not be dealing with this issue still to this day. Yet, here we are, very much needed.

In order to be an effective activist, you need to let go of the misconception that you will completely change the injustice you are fighting against. You will not be able to fix something completely, you will only be able to move the ball down the field a little bit more. Let go of this expectation of yourself and come to a place where there is a realistic outlook on what you can do and accomplish, the reality of what you can change.

Another major misconception in the world of activism is the misunderstanding of peace. We often get the idea in our head that in order for our work to be effective, everything must be completely at peace. There shouldn't be any conflict left, but that everything will be harmonious.

But I would argue that peace does not mean the absence of conflict. We still live in a fallen, sinful world. The absence of conflict is an impossibility right now. Peace is not the absence of conflict, because wherever there are humans there will be conflict.

Peace also does not mean passivity, but an interruption of injustice—it is active. It is a revolution of love that sets both the oppressed and the oppressor free. Peacemaking begins with what we can change: ourselves. It continues in the community and society at large by creative and courageous responses to injustice and violence.

The perfect peace that God can give us is a peace that simply does not exist in this world. The wholeness that He brings into our lives, restoring the brokenness, the injustice, the destruction, is not something that we will see in perfection in our work.

Peace truly is active, though. It is not easy being peacemakers, as fighting can elevate our hearts, emotions, and senses. This is why we don't lean on ourselves, but on what God is doing.

We get glimpses of heaven here on this earth. I think the work that is done to fight injustice is a bit of these glimpses. It is an amazing thing to walk into a situation where there is so much aggression and vitriol contempt and then to be able to see peace break down the walls and a pathway forward sought.

I find being a peacemaker, bringing peace into this world, means that you have to take people who would never want to look at each other and have them sit at the table together. At Amirah, I see peace at work every night at the table during our Community Dinner time.

We often go through seasons where women will be in conflict with one another. When you work through trauma, you tend to take out your emotions and feelings on others. It can be easier than dealing with the pain and hurt that is inside. Bringing peace into this world means that we respect one another enough to break bread together. No matter what has been said, we ask the women to come to the table. There may still be conflict, but that doesn't mean that peace will not exist.

Slowly, we watch as peace interrupts the injustice. We see the offenses forgiven, and we watch the offended person hold the woman who begins to see that her pain is the thing that needs to be addressed. We see hope be restored.

And then we watch this all unfold again and again, week after week. There will always be conflict, but there can also always be peace.

Again, peace is a revolution of love that will set the oppressed and the oppressor free. When I speak of the cycle of sex trafficking, many people want to demonize the traffickers and the buyers. However, if I am going to bring peace and change, I need to hold conflict on this. I don't want to demonize those who are oppressing the women I love so dearly. I want them to be set free as well. Jesus did not just come to die for those who are hurt, but for those who are dishing out the pain as well.

One of the greatest moments of peace that I witnessed was when a woman stood up in court, giving testimony against her trafficker. In her statement, she boldly shared what he had done against her, but then said that she wanted him to come to know the same forgiveness she knew. She wanted him to be healed, because she realized that he was a product of his upbringing as well. He was a part of the cycle of evil. He was culpable for his part, but his sin could still be forgiven. He could still be healed. What beautiful tension this was to witness. Watching peace unfold as we held onto the conflict that justice must be met.

Lastly, I would say that the third misconception you will need to tackle is this: no matter what injustice you are fighting, you will always be a drop in the bucket. Mother Theresa said we have to cast our pebbles out into the water and let the ripples take effect. Mother Theresa said this. Think about that for a minute. She reached millions of people, and she still knew she was just a drop in the bucket.

The misconception, though, is not that you don't already know this—it is that you think your pebble is not doing anything.

If you get the chance to change one life, please go do it. That one life is not alone. That person has parents, friends, cousins and siblings. His or her life is surrounded by more lives. If all you get to do with your time is to change the one life, this will be worth your time.

I often am reminded of the parable of Jesus where He spoke about the shepherd who left the herd of ninety-nine sheep in order to go out and find the one. The shepherd went after the one. When the sheep was found, he rejoiced and celebrated finding it.

One life matters more than we will ever know. Your life mattered more than you will ever grasp. You were that one sheep for the shepherd. I was as well. When I sit back and remember this truth, it makes me happy to pour my life out for one woman at a time. I might only be able to impact her life, but the ripples that go out from there will change her whole community.

The injustice that you fight against might feel overwhelming, but keep casting your pebbles. The work you do today will impact more lives than you will ever fully realize.

With hope, Stephanie

SEVEN

Failing, A Look into Sad Days

What happens when things don't go the way you planned?
—ACTIVIST

Dear Activist:

I'm afraid that this letter will be the hardest one to write to you. There is little cheer on the pages ahead. What you are about to dive into is some raw honesty about the hardest days you will face. It was J. M. Barrie who said, "We are all failures—at least the best of us are." So I am glad to know that I find myself in the "Best of Us" category.

About six weeks after the safe home for Amirah opened, we

lost our first woman who left the safe home program to return to a life on the streets. Six weeks, that was it. She walked away from me down a side alley in Boston, yelling over her shoulder, "How are you going to open up five homes if you can't even help one woman?"

These words sunk in and dug a nice hole in my soul.

My heart was broken. I cried; no, I wept in the car as I drove home that afternoon. She was right. How could I ever expect to open more homes if I couldn't help even one woman? Her words hit me like a semi-truck. They stuck to me like glue, and for a long time, they were a part of me and how I approached this work—taunting me again and again.

Fast-forward three months, and an email was in my inbox. This one was filled with the words: "I wanted to believe that you loved me, but you don't. Thanks for giving up on me." Again, I wept. How could I open more homes if I couldn't even help one woman? Did I give up on her?

There is a phrase in the Bible after the angel Gabriel had just given the virgin Mary the news that she was going to give birth to the Savior of the world. After the angel left, it says, "But Mary treasured up all these things and pondered them in her heart." I think that is exactly what happens for me every time I fail. I don't treasure and ponder the amazing things, the kind words, the words of love—but the words that sting. These words get pondered for days, weeks, months, and in some cases are still getting pondered years later.

As much as I tell myself again and again that these women choose to stay or choose to leave this program on their own accord, part of me doubts this. Failure. With every cutting word they have said or written, this is etched into me. Failure.

How can you open more homes if you can't help even one woman?

The days that follow when a woman leaves, I think and

evaluate. I debrief and rethink again what we are doing. I question our program and the steps we are taking. I question myself and the motives I have. I wake up in the middle of the night and spend the day exhausted as I attempt to get some work done.

Mostly, I think about these women and where they are physically. I pray. If I am honest, those prayers are feeble attempts at best for the circumstances these women are in now. I should be storming the gates of heaven, but all I can do is cry and ask God to protect them.

No one really likes to talk about the fact that working in the anti-trafficking movement means that at best you will have a 30 percent success rate with the victims with whom you work. Those that want to help in this movement begin with the assumption that the help offered is actually wanted. And that is the wake-up call that each of us in this work faces the moment she or he walks away from us, venturing back out into the life, the streets, or some crack house to get a fix.

We will fail. The hope that I see on a woman's face on Tuesday can quickly disappear on Wednesday. No amount of classroom lectures or books (even this one) can prepare you for that moment when everything you have strived for comes crashing down. Nothing prepares you for the warfare that comes your way in the days that follow. Those words get pondered in your heart; they keep you awake at night; they hit you like a bullet time and again as you share in public about the success stories. They do not leave you; they were never meant to.

The only thing I know is that when you fail, your inner self needs something stronger than your own will power. How you discover that strength will look unique to you. Each staff member at Amirah has different ways of dealing with this, so there is no one way to heal that we can offer, as the journey of healing is deeply personal. The reality is that even though we do our best to course-correct and make the next woman's journey a little different, we know we will face the ugly wall of failure again.

I use the word failure because it's honest. I know it may be rubbing many of you wrong by now. I should speak positively. I should talk about how this was the woman's choice. I should talk about the work that was accomplished and the impact that was made in her life. This is all true, and deep down, I know this. But the scary reality is that in the hours and days after something terrible happens, this truth does not come immediately to set you free.

You question and doubt. You seriously doubt. You wonder why you do this work and question if it will even work at all. And you can look deep down and say the truth again and again, but at the end of the day, that is not what will get you through to the next day.

What will get you through is knowing God and having a larger understanding of His love. Paul prayed that the Ephesians would have the *strength* to comprehend how wide and long and high and deep the love of Christ is.[11] The reality is that the more you know and understand and grasp what the love of Christ is, the more you realize the deep wound in the rejection of it. He hands over the kingdom freely, and yet there are those who say, "No, thanks."

This is a quest between you and God—the work of your soul, the journey of faith. It is deeply personal and requires a helping hand along the way, whether that is a friend, spiritual mentor, or even a really good therapist.

The moments of failure expose every part of your life, not to the public, but as you stare in front of the mirror. It feels like your entire being is being ripped apart. The questions and doubts flood in. If you stare in that mirror and cannot see anything on the inside but emptiness, then those doubts become truth rather than lies.

All my time with God is precious, not just the moments of utter despair and failure. In those moments, He is most present, but that is because I have practiced His presence on the days when everything is normal and boring. I'm not perfect in this; I haven't found any secret way to getting to know God. I have just taken up following after Him, reading and discovering truth in His Word, silencing my racing thoughts before His throne of grace, and spending a good deal of time talking to Him about the most inane moments.

This practice shows up in spades on the days when failure rears its ugly head. As I sit there exposed, I realize I am not alone. While every part of me is screaming and yelling at how stupid I have been, telling myself this won't work, that I am a complete failure, He sits there with me, wipes away my tears, and whispers again and again that His "grace is sufficient for me."

The hard reality of the journey inward is that God's grace is indeed sufficient, but we only find this out when we are truly weak. Amazing grace never seems quite as amazing when we are at our best, relishing our proudest moments. Amazing grace is most amazing when we are utterly spent and don't know how we can go on. It is in those moments that we take another step inward and discover the reality of grace, abundant life, and the power He gives to do the work that no human being is ever capable of doing: loving unconditionally those who walk away.

When I speak to people about what we do at Amirah, I get the feeling they envision a beautiful home filled with love, acceptance, and overflowing gratitude. That women come in from the darkest places on earth and are immediately healed because of this place; that their gratitude knows no end, and they immediately start taking the steps needed to start a whole new life.

For anyone who looks from the outside into the world of darkness that is sexual exploitation, it makes absolute sense in our minds that no one would want to stay in that place. No one would want to be raped again and again. No one wants to sell their bodies, be touched over and over, be yelled at, beaten, and drugged.

This is not the reality, though. Victims of exploitation are dealing with substance abuse addictions. They have mental health barriers including post-traumatic stress disorder (PTSD), borderline personality disorder, Stockholm syndrome, bipolar disorder. They are the smartest women you will ever meet, because they have survived in the darkest places you will ever see, but they have also been trained to make choices to survive rather than choices that will help them thrive.

Their emotions have been torn apart, and a square sitting in a beautiful home letting her know that there is food in the kitchen, a warm bed for her, and that we are giving her time and space to heal can be overwhelming. Love is not received freely by them, it is something they feel that they must earn, no matter how much it is freely offered.

So while you sit there in your right mind knowing that you are doing everything you can to offer this woman a path where she can heal and have a life filled with hope, because of everything she is going through in her mind, body, and soul, she can choose to walk away from it all. This does not make sense to someone sitting in my chair. The money that is raised and spent on her feels wasted. The time invested in her, the hours of medical appointments, the hours of phone calls on her behalf, the one-on-one meetings where trust was being built—it is all gone with her choice to return to the darkness.

C. S. Lewis said "that the doors of hell are locked on the inside."[12]

Your job is to wrestle with that. There is no sugarcoating this pain; those days are the hardest days I have ever faced in this work and some of the hardest days I have faced in my life. I have felt like the work I am doing is utterly worthless. I have felt like I have wasted time and money. I have questioned my calling again and again. And that is where the truth comes through. If you are called to do this work, there will be enough grace to do this work. Don't sugarcoat the pain. Feel it, cry through it, walk with the grace that God is giving you through it, because tomorrow is a new day. And the other women that are still in the home and in their program are choosing to walk through their own pain each day. If I can't do the same, then I am in the wrong business.

There are days in this work when I am at my best. I love beyond what I know I am humanly capable of, I treat each person with kindness, even when I am treated with disdain, and I raise ten thousand dollars in a day. Those days are awesome.

And then there are many more days when I am human. My capacity is short, the grumbling and complaining get to me, and I lose it. My voice does not remain calm but gets louder. The hate that is pouring out of her eyes onto me gets reflected right back. These are the days I have to own. I am responsible for the actions and the words I did and said.

There is no way to be perfect in this work. It is draining and exhausting. There is a way to be honest about this work, though. When I mess up, I have to come before the throne of grace and bring my honesty to Him. And then I need to do the same thing to the one who received my wrath. Even if the sentiment was true and right, the actions were not called for. Even those of us who seemingly have it all together mess up.

These are the moments that can stick with you if you don't let grace come in. The thoughts of failure can circle back again and again if you cannot release them and know that grace exists where failure once stood. Grace is the one thing that is hard to receive when we know we have failed. My natural instinct is to take it out on myself. "Of course, I was wrong. Of course this didn't work. Of course she left. You messed up. This is what you deserve." And indeed, that is true. I do deserve the worst. In the world of fair play, if I mess up, I deserve the punishment that comes.

But grace does not live in the world of fair play. Grace is exactly what you don't deserve.

This is why it is the hardest thing to receive. It goes against everything your inner self is saying. It looks at the failures, it looks at the mistakes, it looks at the moments when anger flew freely, and says it is time to learn, know forgiveness, and move forward. This is what a calling is—the ability to receive the grace we know we don't deserve in order to do the work we will mess up at.

Because the truth is that His grace is indeed sufficient.

With hope,
Stephanie

EIGHT

A Policy on Sabbath and Rest

I've seen so many people leave professions they have felt called to for years because they were burned out. How does one prevent this from happening?

—ACTIVIST

Dear Activist:

You know this is one of the questions I get asked the most. How *do* you prevent burnout? I've heard that for people who work in the anti-trafficking movement, particularly in the aftercare area, there is a two-year average before getting burned out. Unfortunately, I've seen it happen as well at Amirah, despite my best efforts to stop it.

At the core of the matter, burnout occurs because boundaries do not exist. Boundaries are difficult to understand, to build up, and to keep in place when you are working in a service or ministry type of setting.

Everyone wants to be like Jesus, so we think we have to say yes to everyone, heal everyone, be there for them at all times, listen to them, and in general, save them. But that is most definitely not what we can do or be. While we know this, when you are in the trenches, it is hard to remember this truth.

Working against injustice in the world can feel overwhelming on the best of days. It drains you and wears you down emotionally. You can become intertwined in someone's pain and hurt in a way that begins to take a stranglehold on your life. And because of this, you begin to put the pain and hurt before everything else in your life. You begin to feel like you are the only one that can help this hurt. You have to be there for it, because if you are not, the hurt will never be healed.

You may be sitting there saying this will never happen to me, and maybe it won't, but I've seen it happen to everyone I have worked with, including myself, at some point or another.

I remember when I was a pastor, I felt this unbelievable urge to be there for parishioners. Sometimes it would get the better of me, though, and I would give my time and effort when I should have been putting up a boundary. For a while, I was the only female pastor on staff, so a good chunk of my ministry was serving and helping women who were going through hard times. The church where I was a pastor was like most churches in America, with women comprising over 50 percent of the congregation. You can imagine then what I was experiencing on a daily basis.

While this sounds challenging, the reality is I really enjoyed this work. I loved sitting with women in pastoral counseling sessions. I loved praying with them at the altar. I loved walking with them through some pretty hard, dark days. But every once in a while, I would have to check myself. Because I began to turn what I loved doing into what I had to do. My ministry became my obligation. My service became my opportunity to save. My boundaries were evaporating when this happened.

So I would pour myself out and serve others. I would sit for hours with one woman and then go back to my office and realize I had a pile of actual work to do as well. I would work more hours than I was asked, all because I felt I had to do this. After a year of displaying poor boundaries and putting this ministry above my family, my husband told me I needed to start to work harder, not longer.

This was a wake-up call for me.

I've rarely held a job where I was not asked to do more work than the hours I had in the day. I think there was only one job once where this didn't happen, and I did not last long there because I ended up bored out of my mind. Even people that work in customer service jobs, where you can supposedly leave your work at work, are still being asked to work overtime or are called in for extra shifts when their coworkers are sick.

We have a problem. Being a workaholic is not new to us. We condemn this from our pulpits, but then somehow when it comes to working with people, doing ministry, being in hands-on compassion activism, we get stretched thin beyond what we should do because this is what Jesus would be doing.

I don't know that He would, though. Jesus did spend an abundant amount of time with people, healing them, serving them, teaching them, loving them. But He also withdrew. He went off alone to pray.[13] He also is God, so I have a really hard time thinking I am going to be perfectly like Him while I am still living in this sinful body here on this earth.

As much as I want to be like Jesus and love like Him, I am going to mess that up.

Every day, I ask my staff to read and meditate on John 15:13: "Greater love has no one than this, that someone lay down his life for his friends."[14] This is the verse that guides us in the work we do. It challenges us on how to love one another and the women we get a chance to serve. It has been difficult to live this verse out and hold the boundaries that are needed for self-care.

I think that is why I picked this verse as the guiding verse for us at Amirah. I want each of us to work through this struggle that is within all of us. This desire to love sacrificially and do that well but then also not put ourselves in a spot where we are unable to function because we have given too much.

Work has received a poor reputation because of workaholics, but the truth I live with each day is that my home life and work life are integrated. When 5:00 p.m. happens, my brain doesn't just shut off and stop thinking about Amirah and the women there. When I wake up at 5:30 a.m., my brain isn't just focused on tea and my Bible; work thoughts begin to roll through. While this could be a bad thing if my focus and sole energy were to turn to work, I think there is a balance one can strike when they have found their calling.

Getting to that sweet spot, though, where the days and work seem to flow seamlessly, can be a bit of a challenge. The greatest advice I can give you is to think on this call to "pray without ceasing."[15] I am not offering you a final answer on what this verse actually means, but I can give you some advice on how to see this happen in your life.

In ministry or the work of activism, the problems are nonstop. The tragedies and trauma stories are heavy loads to bear. Just because you shut your computer down and sit down to dinner, the problems do not stop. When I'm working with someone who is suffering from burnout and compassion fatigue, I hear from them that they wish they could just work a job where they clock out and don't have to think about work after that. Every single person has said this.

What this tells me is that work and life should not be separated but should be integrated in a way that is healthy and balanced. When I end my day, I am still thinking of the women of Amirah. But I switch my problem-solving thoughts into prayers to God. If we are seeing signs in a woman that she may be on the verge of relapse, instead of thinking through the conversations we need to have and the support we need to offer, I change those thoughts into prayers to God about those conversations. I ask Him to give us the strength to support her. And then I give this woman to Him.

I don't let my thoughts turn into worry. I make them into prayers. Pretty soon, I have a release from them, and I am going about my evening and time with my family. This practice is not easy. I wish I could tell you that I have it mastered and have found the secret to work-life balance. But there are still days I fail miserably at this. Those days are the reminder to me that while Jesus is my amazing example, this earth is still fallen and broken.

I don't know if we give that enough thought: the brokenness of this world. When I am wrestling and struggling to find the balance between work and life, I often have this longing to find rest. I become so tired that even when I do rest, I am not refreshed. I realized through the years that I was not the only one who had this struggle at times in their work. I was seeing my staff struggle, and I saw a few of them burn out.

Because I believe in supporting staff as a top priority, I wrote up a "Policy on Sabbath and Rest" that guides us at Amirah. Yes, we have a policy on rest. I have not heard of many places that do this, but it felt necessary to say some things I knew in my heart.

We often hear mixed messages, especially when it comes to work-life balance. Our bosses and leaders tell us to "go home" or "take a vacation," but then they call us after-hours or when we are on the beach in Hawaii. This can be frustrating.

What happens when we actually do go home or take the vacation, but we still don't get that rest because our time of rest is filled with other stressors? Work is not the only stress in life; family can be as well. So when we are done with work for the day, we are supposed to be finding rest and time of break with our family, whether you live with them or not. But they could be providing added stress to your time of rest.

I have two preteenage daughters in my home. I can tell you there is very little rest after I end my day at Amirah. My Sabbath day is not really a day, so much as moments throughout a day.

We have to realize and recognize that any Sabbath we rest in now will still be broken rest. But this does not mean God cannot honor the Sabbath we take and restore the brokenness of sin in this world.

I have found that God honors the boundaries I put in place when I keep my priorities in check. Loving unconditionally only works if you begin your love with Him. Being loved by God and filled with His love starts this entire beautiful journey. Our response is to love God back, but when you work to help and serve others, their needs and wants can often begin to take first place.

So the love I am supposed to pour back out to God who loved me first gets redirected and used up by the pressings needs of the traumatized. The reality is this will drain me every time. Holding the trauma of another person is draining. It is tiring. It is impossible to do if that is your first priority, because trauma will take everything out of you and keep asking for more. It doesn't know when to stop, it just wants to be needed.

God doesn't need us, though. While that sounds harsh, I hope you can see the amazing release and peace in that. God doesn't need my love in order to survive; He just delights in it. When I am honest with myself, that is my heart's desire: to have someone delight in the love I give. Our Creator does that.

If you place your priority with God first, then loving unconditionally becomes natural and boundaries feel good, not like you are failing someone.

After you fix your eyes on God, the second priority is your family. It is a cliché that ministry families take a backseat to parishioners. The same is true in the world of activism. The needs of the traumatized are often pushed above the time for our families. This shouldn't be the case, and we need to stop making places of work that don't value families.

I have found it disheartening that when I see staff members go through a personal crisis, they are surprised when I want to support them, give them extra time off, and call to see how things are going. It shows we have a problem in this world, when we talk about putting families first, but the reality is this has become empty talk.

Make your family and friends a priority. Shut things down at the end of your forty hours. Put those spinning thoughts into confident prayers and be with your family. Read to your kids, laugh with your spouse, spend time with your friends, go for walks or bike rides, take time to be together. If you do the normal things well, then when the draining times come, you will more easily love your family unconditionally as well.

God first, family second, calling last. This is the philosophy of work at Amirah: those we are hired to help come last on our list. It sounds so counterintuitive, but it is what sustains us.

Prioritizing what God wants and placing boundaries where they are needed.

I speak often of boundaries to people in the human services field. The hardest lesson we each learn is that a boundary is not only for our protection, but also for those we are helping. It builds them up emotionally. It supports them personally. It allows them a chance to grow, to fail, to stumble, but to be supported in a healthy way, not in a damaging way.

Offering support with no boundaries is dangerous. It endangers your mental health, it puts your family's safety in jeopardy, and it causes pain and confusion rather than building up confidence and independence. Boundaries will not harm others; they will help them and restore you.

With hope, Stephane

NINE

Support the Hobbits

How do you find the right people to do this work?
—ACTIVIST

Dear Activist:

One of the greatest joys I have in my job is when I am invited to speak to college students. I love being able to engage with the future generation about this work, but more than that, about life, how to find balance, how to discover your passion, how to figure out what to do with your life. So many great questions are asked during those times when I sit with young, inspiring minds.

At one gathering, I was asked a fun question meant to bring insight:

If I could be any character from the fellowship in The Fellowship of the Ring, *who would I be?*

Now, I must say that I absolutely love this question, as I am a bit of a LOTR nerd. Of course, anyone who is asked such an important question wants to come across as both humble and noble; most would probably pick Samwise, the loyal friend who helped carry the ring to destruction. However, I smiled and said, "I would be Aragorn."

Yes, the king—I would be the king. Not exactly a statement of humility. Once the declaration of pride settled down on the group, I took a moment to explain my choice. You see, I am the face of a nonprofit organization. I am the one who gets the phone calls from reporters; I am asked to speak to groups about this issue; I am the one hugged and prayed for and cried to and thanked over and over again. People look at me and somehow think I am the one saving these women that come into our safe home. (FYI, no one is saving these women except God).

The reality is that I am merely the king. At the end of the trilogy, when (*spoiler alert*) evil is defeated, King Aragorn stands before his people. The crowd bows down before their king, including the four hobbits that sacrificed everything to see evil destroyed. Aragorn stops the hobbits from making the gesture of respect and honor and says through tears, "My friends, you bow before no one."[16]

This, in my humble opinion, is one of the greatest pictures of leadership: the recognition of those who sacrifice everything in secret and the reality that you would not be where you are without them. While I am the face of Amirah, I am not the one putting in the incredibly hard hours of work with the traumatized women that come into our safe home. I am not the one who gets the phone calls on weekends because a woman is having a panic attack. I am not the one who sits with a woman as she comes to the realization that the man she thought was her boyfriend really was her pimp. I am not the one who hears the stories of trauma. While I fight this evil, I am not continually exposed to it each day, nor am I the one to navigate the complex world of trauma, addiction, and psychological hurdles these women face.

My staff are my hobbits. They quietly walk into the land of Mordor and up Mount Doom each day. Most people don't know their names or faces. Most people have no idea the amount of work they do each day for a woman. They don't receive the hugs or the notes of encouragement. Quite the opposite in fact, because most days they receive complaints. Yet they get up each day and do this work.

Finding these women that work for me was probably one of the hardest things I have ever had to do, mostly because I didn't expect how hard it would be. You write up a job description and think it should be a no-brainer that the right person will just naturally apply to do this incredibly difficult job. Who wouldn't want to do this work that takes so much of who you are? Who wouldn't want to work for a boss that is type A and goal driven?

I soon found out how hard this would be when I went to hire the key piece for our staff, the program director. I knew that for me to be able to do my job, I needed a program director who would collaborate with me, but not need me. Essentially, the safe home would be hers, the organization would be mine. The number of résumés that came in once the job was posted was a bit overwhelming. The overwhelming feeling soon switched to disappointment as résumé after résumé revealed inexperience. I'm all for people reaching for the stars, but I wasn't expecting so many people who had zero experience in trauma, addiction recovery, and mental health to apply.

This is what happens when you work in the world of

anti-trafficking. Callings and desires to become saviors trump the understanding that expertise in trauma-recovery is needed to lead a program. Thankfully, through the stacks of résumés showing passion but lack of experience, I found my right arm, an incredible woman named Heather. When I told her I needed her to tell me how to run the safe home and program, she came back with a PowerPoint presentation. When I asked her in the job interview what she would need, she said, quite intuitively, "I need support. There will be many days I will question what I am doing, so I just need an ear to listen and an affirmation that this is indeed good work." That was how this all began.

My responsibility is to the staff. If they are unable to do their jobs well, then I am not doing my job in leading them. I like to call this "supporting the hobbits." We often hear the word *sustainability* used in the world of activism. To run an organization, you must have sustainable funding. But for the organization to run well, the work and programs must prove to be sustainable—meaning that human beings must be able to do the work that is required.

As I have mentioned before, as activists we tend to idealize and dream big. The systems and perfect worlds we create in our heads as we combat incredible evils sound wonderful. Solutions on paper can look easy, but the reality is that human capabilities can often wreck our perfect paper solutions. As much as I envision myself to be Wonder Woman, I have no superhuman strength or abilities. I am a mere mortal, and those that work for me are just the same.

Supporting your staff is quite possibly one of the most important things you can do as a leader. Making sure they don't constantly feel questioned, watched, and micromanaged, but instead are given space to be able to say they need a break; that something in the perfect system is not working; that more support might actually be needed.

It sounds counterintuitive, right? We are supposed to be driven, work hard, find a way to suck it up and get it done. But the more I work in the world of activism and specifically the human services field, the more I realize we are limited not just by resources, but by the very nature of who we are as human beings. We were not designed to be the saviors of the world, and we are most dangerous to ourselves and to others when we try to be.

There is so much more to this, which I will unpack in later letters, because there is truth and good measure in hard work, and there is also the needed ability to balance life with work; but for the purposes of this letter, I want to focus on the ability to recognize the capabilities of those you work with or those who work for you.

Most days I can sit back and watch my staff do some extraordinary work. But the reality is that for us to make any sort of dent in this world of anti-trafficking aftercare, we must know our limits and allow others to pick up when we are not able to continue.

As a driven, multitasking leader, I tend to schedule more things into my day than there are hours. Some mornings, I set out a list of twenty things and think I can accomplish all of them before my first meeting at 10:00 a.m. On those mornings, I usually look up at the clock at 9:45 and scream out in frustration that the time has magically disappeared as I stare at the seven remaining things on my list. But I deal with spreadsheets, communication, and projections most days.

My staff deal with trauma. A spreadsheet may tire your eyes and sap your brainpower, but there is nothing quite like working with complex trauma that can drain you to your core physically, mentally, emotionally, and spiritually. I found this out one year the week between Christmas and New Year's. In our second season of holidays, I tried very hard to give the staff as much time off as they needed. So we loaded up the safe home with volunteers, and I became the staff member that was physically present and on call. It should have been a somewhat easy week since almost everyone was off, so appointments didn't happen, and schedules were light.

For some reason, I thought that with the "light week," I would be able to do the basic function of running the safe home, working with the women there, and get a few of my projects done. I foolishly thought this, because as the leader, I have that tendency to think I can always do more than most. Let the hubris continue to raise its ugly head. By the second day, I shut my laptop and realized there was absolutely no way any part of my work was going to get done, because I was, to put it simply, wiped. My emotional capacity had been weighed and found wanting.

The business world is driven by production: if one person is found to be producing less than someone else, he or she is cut, and someone with more production power is put in that place. But those of us in the world of fighting evil cannot be driven by production, but by capacity. What are we actually capable of doing? Am I the person that can handle hearing the stories of rape, sexual assault, and slavery? How do I hear those stories and then write a report or send an email about a volunteer opportunity ten minutes later?

Even those of us who grew up with high hopes and huge dreams of how we would change the world get a rude wake-up call when we step into this work. The perfect worlds designed on paper fade away as we realize we must figure out how we can sustain this; how I can get up each day and do this again and again? You have to figure this out for yourself, but if you are the leader, you also have to guide those under you to do the same.

You have to lead them by supporting them, lifting them up, and providing for their needs so they can reach their capacity in the work they do.

There is an incredible sacrifice that happens each day when my staff walk into their offices. Most days, I am not asking what they accomplished, but I do ask how they are doing. At our debrief and connect meetings, I make sure they know I hear their pain. I listen to the words they have had to take in from the survivors, I hear the struggles and questions about their value and worth, and I affirm who they are and the work they are called to do.

Support the hobbits. It might take them far longer to get to Mordor than you expected, but the reality is one does not simply walk into Mordor.

With hope, Stephanie

TEN

Working Together

How do you know who to collaborate
with, and how do you do it well?
—ACTIVIST

Dear Activist:

I have heard it said before that in the United Kingdom, when someone becomes passionate about an issue and seeks to make a difference, they will go out and find an organization that is already doing the work they want to help in and get involved. They will not reinvent the wheel or begin their own nonprofit organization. Instead, they will choose to find the current experts and pour out their time, resources, talents, and treasure.

I'm not sure what it is about the stubborn American will, but in the United States, I find we do the exact opposite. We become passionate about an issue, and instead of looking to see who is in the field and offering our help, we form a 501(c)(3) and claim our territory. Better yet, I've had people who come to help us for a time at Amirah just so they can get a look at our materials, because they want to go start their own thing and thought this was the best way they could go do that.

I wish I could wave a magic wand over this issue and make it all go away, but this will not happen. People will always think they have the best solution, that their way will be the best way, and that they have to stake their claim. My hope, though, is that after you read this, you will stop filling out your tax identification forms for a moment and instead begin to do some research on who is in your area right now who you could get involved with.

I never imagined that when I became an activist one of the hardest challenges I would face is the competition that is present among organizations and activists. I've sat in meetings with over thirty different organizations in the anti-trafficking movement in Boston. At each meeting, we go around the circle and each report what has been happening in our organizations. By the end, it feels like we all had to one-up one another on how much good we were doing. Activism should not be a competition to do better in order to outshine someone else; yet somehow this has crept into our work. We have begun to think that our good actions will outweigh someone else's.

I'm not sure where all of the competition has come from, but I know part of it stems from a lack of resources and funding. Nonprofits are in constant competition over grants, federal funding, and even donors. We try to produce the best numbers possible in order to show that donor money will be invested and spent well; that every dollar is resourced to its full potential, and that the model someone is supporting is the best, most proven, most effective one there is.

This is pressure. No wonder we have to constantly be on the top, trying to one-up one another.

But I want to talk to you about a different way today. A few years ago, I received a phone call from a man named Charles. His call came after a month where I had been called upon by five different organizations that were attempting to start a safe home in the New England region. They were calling us because we were the experts in this field, and they wanted to learn how to do this well. I try hard to be a collaborator and not a competitor, so I will always talk with someone who is trying to start up a safe home in order to help them do it well. However, at the end of every conversation, I point out to them that if they don't want to start this thing up from scratch, they could instead support Amirah, and we will work on coming to their area to duplicate and produce another Amirah safe home program.

As I mentioned, I had received five phone calls within a month about this issue. I made my pitch to every person that called, but no one took my offer.

Charles gave me a call, letting me know he was from a task force in Connecticut that had formed to start a safe home. At this time, there were no safe homes in the state of Connecticut for survivors of sex trafficking, and they wanted to be a part of the change by bringing a safe home there.

We chatted for about an hour, and at the end of the conversation, Charles agreed it was a smarter move on their part to partner with someone else who was already doing this work, rather than to try to start from scratch on their own. Six months later, Charles and another from the task force came for a site visit to see what we really were all about. They toured our facility, talked with our staff, and sat with Heather, our program director, and I for lunch.

We chatted about our challenges and dreams. We talked about the hard lessons we had learned while working with this population of women. We emphasized that while we felt like we knew what we were doing, we still had a long way to go. We were honest about our areas of failure and about our areas where we knew we needed to grow and get better. At the end of the lunch, we left with an idea that it would be better to come together than to continue to work alone.

A partnership began to form. This task force was under the umbrella of a nonprofit in Connecticut called "The Underground," led by two amazing women named Annmarie and Theresa. They had been doing awareness about the issue of sex trafficking for five years already throughout the whole state. They were well connected and were working to connect churches to organizations that were in this work. Their biggest heart was to get the church to be the hands and feet in the anti-trafficking movement in Connecticut. It is a beautiful mission, one that invites collaboration and squashes out competition.

They welcomed Amirah to the table with open arms. They listened to the challenges we faced and began to help us with the solutions. Then, when it came time for us to duplicate, they became the voice in Connecticut for us. They championed the work that was being done and helped us to cast the vision for where we were headed. They said over and over again, "We don't want to start a safe home, we want to bring one here."

I never once felt like they were stepping into my lane; instead, I felt like they were pushing us along and running with us.

Collaboration, not competition.

Have you ever given thought to the challenge that Nehemiah faced? Here is a man who is facing insurmountable odds. He returned to the ruined city of Jerusalem with its city walls and gates destroyed. They were essentially sitting ducks. Any army could march in at any time and continue to plumage and take what they wanted. Without a city wall and gates, there was no chance for the people of Israel to begin to restore their lives in the city of Zion.

Chapter three of Nehemiah is one of the most beautiful pictures of collaboration. Go through it and count all of the times you see the phrase "next to them." They saw a problem and decided to work together. Every person had their lane, their job, their work they had to do, but when you put one's work up next to another's, it became the pieces of the huge puzzle to solve the problem of the destroyed wall.

How do you know who to collaborate with? Well, a big part of this is prayer. Pray about who you need to work with. Pray that God would bring other people into your life and into the life of your organization who will help it to grow and further its mission. Once this is done, start to open yourself up to the possibility that God will actually answer this prayer.

I had been praying for years that we would open up another safe home, I just had no idea how this was going to happen. Thankfully, God brought Charles, Annmarie, and Theresa into my life.

It is important to be at the table with like-minded people, but it is also important to be at the table with people who will challenge you and help you to grow. As activists, we can tend to get stuck in our silos. We work hard and devise solutions for a living, so it is difficult to listen to others when they want to chime in with solutions to our problems.

What does it take to do collaboration well? Collaboration

takes humility. It's hard to be called an expert in a field and then be asked to become humble. I get the irony. But if you want to become a great collaborator, then you need to desire humility. We don't have all of the answers. We cannot do all of the work. There truly must be a place at the table for all of us to sit together and do this work together.

Instead of having these huge meetings where we chime in with how much work we are accomplishing, I wish that we would have meetings where we would come together and lay out one big problem that is in the reach of all of us solving. The problem needs to be big enough that one of us alone would not be able to do it with our resources, time, and talent, but that together, the problem could be annihilated.

I think this is what happened with the Underground Task Force. They saw the problem: there are no safe homes in Connecticut. They invited more people to the table: collaboration, not competition. They gave out practical steps to everyone: a solution was found, and practical work was accomplished.

No one was worried about the funding. When the time came for funds to be needed, there was not competition over these funds. This is the beautiful thing when you have your sight focused on the will of God—the problem of funds becomes rather small because you realize you are dealing with the bank account of the heavenly Father, who always provides more than we could ever ask or imagine.

I've never felt less frustrated and more at ease than when I am working in collaboration with someone else. We can go so much further together than we can trying to tackle all of the problems alone. There is far too much injustice in the world for just you to take it on by yourself.

So what can you do to change your mind-set? Who can you

find that is already doing the work you desire to do? Trust me, they are out there, and they could use your support. If they are anything like me, they will value it and be grateful for it. I don't want to do this work alone; I want amazing people walking with me. I want so many more of us out there fighting against this evil, not fighting against one another.

With hope, Stephanie

ELEVEN

The Rhythm of Grace

What is it like to offer someone a
chance to change their life?

—ACTIVIST

Dear Activist:

I am a big fan of the idea and notion of the "rhythm of grace." There is a wonderful worship song so entitled that speaks mountains to this idea. But my favorite vision of this idea comes from Psalm 19. "The heavens declare the glory of God; the skies proclaim the work of His hands."[17] Whenever I hear this song, I envision nature singing out to God and to us all about how amazing He is.

Picture the most beautiful sunrise in your mind. Do you see

it? You woke up at some hour you never imagined possible just to hike a mountain and reach the top. And as you sit down, the sun begins to crest over the foothills. Shimmers of orange and pink stretch out revealing the infinite horizon below you. Rays shoot through the clouds falling down on the treetops of green.

The darkness is overwhelmed by color and light. As you feel the warmth on your face and breathe in the morning air, you can almost hear the faint sound of melody and harmony rushing over you. His creation sings out with everything that it is. It's the rhythm of grace, the welcoming to a brand-new day where God says His mercies are new for you.

It can be an amazing experience to be a part of this in God's creation. It is so clear and evident when you do get to see His beauty at work, the paint strokes of His brush in the sky—there is an overwhelming joy that rushes through you, the realization that you don't deserve this much beauty and yet here it is being given for you to enjoy. What grace!

As an activist, you have the chance to be caught in the rhythm of grace through action and what you do. If I may say so, this may very well be the best reason of all to become an activist. The thing I have learned about grace over my years is that it is amazing to receive, and because of my sinful heart, it takes real, hard, concentrated effort to give.

Grace is given. It is not deserved, it is not earned, it is not based upon points or merit. It is given freely to one and all. What exactly is it though?

I think that grace has a few different attributes. Love is deep in there. The idea of a second chance, maybe the third, fourth, fifth, twentieth chance. It is taking the wrong and throwing it as far away as possible. Favor—more than just a simple, "I like you, so I am going to bless you," but a deep and profound gift, something that means something to the person receiving it. It is choice. It is specialized. It is hearing the whispered words of love, "I have loved you with an everlasting love. I am yours, and you are mine."

I remember the moment I received grace from God in my life. I was seventeen and had spent part of spring break with some Bible-thumping Christian Baptists. I prayed some prayer and "gave my life to Christ," but in my heart I had plans to spend the rest of the weekend binge drinking my pain and hurt away. When I came back from this experience, something inside of me nudged and said, "Go visit Beth."

Beth was a good friend of mine. She was a Christian, which I had not held against her. She was kind, and fun, and we made awesome cookies together whenever we were going through heartbreak over a stupid boy who wouldn't return our affections. I drove to her home that day instead of heading home right away.

When I pulled into her driveway, she was just arriving home herself. She had been spending her spring break working at a local animal shelter. We said hi, and she began to ask about my time away with the Baptists. I scratched my head and said what I thought I needed to say. That, well, you see, this thing happened last night, and well… "Beth, I'm saved." I didn't really know what was happening, but Beth came and gave me a huge hug. And then she just kept hugging me. It was one of those deep hugs where the person just holds you and showers you with love.

I let out a sigh, and with it, the idea of going out partying. The pain I had felt, the years of hurt, the hate in my heart, the anger, the rejection, all of it just melted away. It was in that moment I knew, I knew that this thing I had done wasn't just for this special week away. It wasn't just meant for a weekend; it was going to be my life. This was my life—living in this grace.

This grace was just for me. It was exactly what I needed, never knowing how much I needed it. It put love in my life when all I had was anger. It put possibilities in my future that had never been there before. It changed everything.

Grace was given to me again and again. It still is given over and over again today. Love, favor, amazing moments that I never realized I needed—it is given freely. It is true what John writes, that "from His fullness we have all received, grace upon grace."[18]

But we do not live this life just to receive grace. Grace, once received, must be given out. We cannot just hold on to love selfishly and expect that this is how life should be lived. When you give out grace, I find that doing this the first time can be a bit of a rush. It feels really amazing to simply bless someone and love them in a special way. It is often hard to do, as grace is usually tied to some sort of forgiveness, but once it is done, it is beautiful.

You are caught up in the rhythm of grace. You are caught up in the moment and start to be a part of this great, huge, divine work. The rhythm of grace begins to take hold of your life. I like to call this the heartbeat of God. One of my favorite passages of scripture comes from 2 Corinthians 4. This is the chapter where Paul is describing what it is like to be a missionary and juxtaposes so eloquently that they "are afflicted in every way, but not crushed; perplexed, but not driven to despair; persecuted, but not forsaken; struck down, but not destroyed…"[19]

This chapter, for me, is the quintessential explanation of the heart of God. It has the bookend from Paul that "we do not lose heart," with him explaining to start that they will not lose heart, then unleashing what it is like to live within the rhythm of grace, and finishing off with the firm stance, "So, we do not lose heart."[20] When you read through it, you feel this pace—for me, I literally feel a heartbeat. There is a cadence to reading these words; there is emotion, there is raw honesty.

The work of grace giving is hard. Paul doesn't mince words on this. He has been afflicted in every way possible. He has sat and pondered and been perplexed. He has been persecuted. He has been struck down. But nothing stops him, because he knows that nothing stops God.

This is the heartbeat that keeps going. He does all of this so that "grace extends to more and more people."[21]

Ah, and there it is. Grace goes out again and again. It doesn't stop. It has a rhythm of its own. Persecution will not stand in its way. Being perplexed and left not understanding will not stop it. Grace will still go out. It is always going out. You just have to have the obedience to be a part of that rhythm.

Working with survivors of sex trafficking has been the hardest work I have ever done. There have been more nights of lying awake at 3:00 a.m. praying to God that He would change the life of a woman than I care to mention. There have been hard conversations where I sit there offering a woman life and then she ends up choosing death. I have been perplexed more times than I care to admit, but I will not be driven to despair.

There is only so much that we can do with the women that come into our safe home. They are with us for about two years, which to some people sounds like an eternity. So much could be accomplished, right? Yet, because of trauma, we measure accomplishments in inches, not in miles. Did a woman wake up in the morning on time? That is a huge inch of growth. Did she come to a staff member and clearly tell her that she was struggling with depression? Another huge inch of growth. Did she fill out a job application for the first time in her life? Man, that is like six inches of growth.

Our goal is to help them start their journey of liberation.

For anyone who has had to work through trauma, you know that healing is a never-ending journey in this life. We do our absolute best to help them get a sure foothold for this journey they will be taking, but we don't get to address everything. Because of trauma, trust has to be built. Trust is something that happens over the course of weeks and months, and really, just about the time you think something has taken ahold, that is when they are graduating and moving out on their own to try their hand at life.

When a woman graduates Amirah, we don't force ourselves on them, but we offer as much support as we can give and as much as they want. They still stumble, they still make stupid choices, they still make me have nights where I sit there perplexed. I remember talking with my husband one night about a woman who had graduated our program. She was in a relationship with a man, after having gone through two very bad relationships and despite our advice and support to live life single for a while as she worked on her healing journey. So to hear that she was in, yet again, another relationship was a bit of a blow. Dave looked at me and shook his head. "I don't know how you keep doing this."

I chuckled and said, "Because this is what God is doing."

And this is where the truth of grace comes in—it doesn't stop. It continues to go out again and again. It is this beautiful dance that God is unfolding here on this earth, and either you jump in and join the dance, or you wallow in despair. This work is hard; this work will take every bit of what you have to offer; but it won't take everything. We do not lose heart. God hasn't, so we don't either.

With hope, Stephanie

TWELVE

Aiming at Heaven

What drives you to stay in this work?

—ACTIVIST

Dear Activist:

How do you feel about C. S. Lewis? I find there are two camps of thought about this man. Either you love him and want his writing to invade every part of your life, or you don't get what all the fuss is about. My husband happens to lie in the second camp, whereas I am firmly in the former. I am one of those typical Christians who manages to throw a Lewis quote into almost all of her writings, sermons, and simple daily musings. Part of me wishes I was original, but then I pick up a Lewis book and realize I have found a soulmate. So

I have come to the conclusion I will not be ashamed of my love for this man.

One of the things I love about Lewis is his retelling of his faith journey, going from agnostic to theist to Christian. I found one of the most heart-tugging lines in his book *Surprised by Joy* was when he described what happened when a hardened atheist remarked about the evidence for Christ. Lewis recalls the atheist's words, "Rum thing, all that stuff of Frazer's about the Dying God. Rum thing. It almost looks as if it had really happened once."[22]

Rum thing indeed, Mr. Lewis. The Dying God—the God who loved the world so much that He gave up Himself for it. The God who sacrificed and said this is love. The God who then said, "Okay, I've shown you what love is. Now go do as I did and teach others to do the same. Go, I'll be with you. Just go and love—love like I did."

I have spent a good amount of time in my life reflecting on this rum thing, this Dying God. I meditate each morning His words that tell me that "greater love has no one than this then one lay down His life for His friends."

That simple truth frightens me and challenges me. It frightens me, because if I study myself and dive into the heart of who I truly am, I am so far from these words it is almost laughable. What frightens me even more is that the more I read writings by the people I respect the most, the more I see the same sentiment coming from them. Mother Theresa and Lewis both had this stark truth of themselves, that this command to love was all they should desire to seek, and yet they both felt so far from it.

It feels impossible to love like this because this world can feel so heavy and evil at times. Watching the endless news cycle of who is bombing who, what active shooter situation is happening, hundreds of girls being kidnapped in some remote country, tsunamis that wipe out whole cities—it is too much. Too much evil, too many horrible things happening all at once, too much being cycled through again and again.

I remember when the Twin Towers were hit. I was sitting in Old Testament Survey at Moody Bible Institute in Chicago. Dr. Marty was in the middle of his lecture when someone came in to stop the class. We were asked to stay on campus, but we were not allowed to go above three floors, so my dorm room on the fourth floor became off limits. As I sat in the commons, I watched the news loop the footage of the plane tearing through the first building. And then, as the buildings fell, they suddenly had new footage to loop.

I remember being numb and sick to my stomach that day. I couldn't stand seeing the footage on repeat, so I walked around the city feeling lost and uncertain. We live in a world where we watch evil unfold on repeat. We get live updates and video feeds on social media. The worst of humanity is on display now for all of the flat world to see.

This can be overwhelming. How do we cope? How do we deal? Evil is a very real thing I fight against every day in the work we do at Amirah. We hear the stories of horror from women's lips; we watch as some relapse and choose to go back to the cycle of exploitation; we hold on to the trauma of another, somehow hoping that when God says we are supposed to bear one another's burdens, He really knew and understood what that meant.

I find we cannot talk about how to love people if we do not talk about the evil we face. Most days, I have no problem loving my husband. He is simply the best gift I have ever been given. He is easy to love, even on days I am mad at him. You know what is not easy to love? Someone who is spitting vitriol venom in your face.

I think the world we live in now, for as tolerant as it wants to be, is far too engrossed in how evil and wrong everything is rather than in showing unconditional love. I hear more news stories about what is wrong with the world than about what is happening that is good. As those stories of tragedy play on repeat, we are then treated to a barrage of analysis bylines, where reporters nitpick at everything that is going wrong, why it is wrong, and how much damage this is going to do.

When a story of hope comes along, it might get five minutes of air time in a twenty-four-hour news cycle. It seems crazy, but the reality is hope doesn't sell. People are somehow drawn to the tragedy.

I would like to challenge this and be a part of the change to this. Hope might not sell in the news cycle, but it is what I want my life to be about. The funny thing about hope is that it can only begin to exist because unconditional love is being shown. The two are tied together.

The rum thing about this is that the best place to learn about unconditional love is in the greatest sacrifice and tragedy of all—the Dying God who gave Himself up for those who reject Him. Dying for friends is an ideal notion most of us would say we would be willing to do, but dying for someone who is still spitting in our faces seems impossible.

Greater love has no one than this, than one who lay down his life for his friends. Except, the Dying God didn't just stop at His friends. He did it for everyone.

This is the greatest glimpse I think we get into heaven. A God who loves me so much that even if I reject Him, He will still come chasing after me and give Himself up for me. When I feel worthless and utterly stuck in myself, I am reminded there is a God who loves me and pursues me still. He is relentless in His gift of grace.

When this reality hits you, it changes everything. I have spent most of my life now in pursuit of understanding this incredible love. The more you pursue unconditional love, the more hope builds up inside of you. It's just simple heaven logic. The more hope I have, the more I reject the evil cycle of this world and start to bring what I call pockets of heaven down here.

There is a phrase in the Lord's Prayer that has always caught my attention. It is the one that ends the beginning part of the prayer by saying, "On earth as it is in heaven." Whatever is happening in heaven, God, we want it here on earth too. Your will, Your kingdom, Your holy name—bring it here.

And yet, the news cycle continues. More earthquakes, more politicians, more nuclear tests, more death. If I focus on the endless progression of death, I will be led into despair. Don't you agree?

I think this is the great mystery of how all these commands and prayers come together. Sacrificial love, dying for those who reject you, offering love in the face of persecution and anger, bringing heaven to this earth—little pockets of heaven.

Part of the greatest steps in faith is the understanding that there is another world yet to come. One where there is no endless cycle of tragic news stories, but instead is filled with joy and wonder and some pretty good awe.

The good days are when I get to catch glimpses of that in the life I lead here and now. The best days are when I get to be a part of bringing that pocket of heaven to earth myself.

When I first met Jessie, she was a bit standoffish, to say the least. She wore her sunglasses at all times as a blocker from having to eye-to-eye with someone. She said no to almost any request. She had a big wall of protection up and was in fight-or-flight mode. The first time I spoke to her on the phone, she hung up on me because she didn't know who I was. There is nothing more affirming for you in your job than to have someone you are attempting to love hang up the phone on you.

As the weeks unfolded, I put into practice the meditation of my heart—lay down my life and love this woman. So I laid down my pride and hurt feelings, I laid down my lofty goals and dreams, and I came to her space with humility and offered her love. After a few weeks, her sunglasses were off. Another week passed, and we were laughing together.

Then Christmas came, and she went into her shell again. It's one of the hardest things to watch when the season of life and light means death to someone else. But I loved, I prayed, I waited. By the end of the season, she was asking me questions that I could have only dreamt about.

Why do you stick with this, Steph? Why are you doing this for me?

So I shared with her about the someone who loved me when I didn't feel lovable. And then she asked me if she could come to church with me.

She came, she experienced, she cried and wept, and then she began to ask a thousand questions. The thing I have learned when you are in the middle of watching a pocket of heaven come to this earth is if you attempt to rush this process, you will utterly destroy it. Patience and timing that is divine; this is what you need to look for.

So I didn't shove Romans roads down her throat. I let her ask her questions and did my best to answer. At the end I asked if she wanted to come back next week, and she said yes. Another week, another experience, another Sunday of tears and questions. This would happen two more times.

The fourth Sunday, I noticed there was something different about her. The tears were still there, but the questions were dying away. A nudge inside of me said she was ready for the answer. And here is where being a part of the pocket of heaven is one of the greatest joys you will ever get to experience.

I asked her at the end of the service what she wanted to pray about, and she responded, "Steph, I don't want to be bought and sold anymore."

The nudge again, the beauty of the answer.

"That's amazing, Jess. Because Jesus bought you and He will never sell you."

And there, right in front of her, is the answer, the unconditional love she has been searching for her entire life.

The amazing thing is that when you aim at heaven in your life, the endless cycle of evil melts away. Don't get me wrong, I am deeply saddened by the evil in this world, but I am not driven to despair, and I am not driven by this evil to do something. I am driven by hope, by the pockets of heaven I get to see. I am driven by love.

What is driving you, my dear activist?

With hope,
Stephanie

THIRTEEN

Taking the Leap

How did you get into this work?
—ACTIVIST

Dear Activist:

This is a question I get asked at every speaking engagement I do. How did I get into this work? One time, a woman came up to me while I was manning a booth for Amirah and asked me this. It was a crowded space, so I needed to give her my five-second answer. I let her know that my faith in God that was what led me to do this work. She replied, "Well, I'm an atheist, but if He told you to do this, that's great!" I still laugh about that conversation to this day.

The short answer is God. He is always the answer, it seems.

But the reality is that being an activist and working in the world of anti-trafficking was a lifelong journey that God led me on. I'm sure the same can be said for so many people out there. We have markers along the way that we can look back on and realize were the nudges that God was giving us.

As I mentioned before, I do not regret any of the years that led me to this work. They were formative and a part of the will of God for my life. I find that when you get a glimpse of the will of God, it is this incredibly peace-filled place. Most of the time, though, we get that glimpse in hindsight, and then we realize the peace that we had during the entire process.

I became a follower of Jesus when I was seventeen. I had high aspirations at that time of becoming a business owner and making a lot of money. I wanted to be a restaurant owner. I was a visual, artistic person, so I had these grand visions in my head about what these restaurants would look like. But after I became a Christian, things began to change.

I had a hard time picturing my future as a business owner. I couldn't see it. Slowly, as I read through scripture and spent time in prayer, I began to see a brighter vision for my future. Quite literally, it was a bright vision. It was a perfect sunset over a broad horizon, and I had the greatest sense of peace I had ever had in my life. I didn't know what it meant. I didn't have some audible voice saying, "Go to Africa;" I just knew I needed to follow God and He would get me there.

So I enrolled in Bible college and let my home church know that I would like to pursue ministry, blurting out that I would like to help women. I don't know why I said that, but I did. They happened to be launching a program for single women missionaries to go over to Northern Africa and work with Muslim women. You had to be a single woman in order to do this type of work because of the cultural boundaries. I signed up and went off to college to get some training. My plans were set; I was going to go to Libya in four years.

And then a man named Dave came along and changed my plans.

He was the happiest change to my plans. Dave has been and continues to be my rock. He has supported me through this process of figuring things out. When I told him in shock that I was going to be a published author, he kindly let me know he was not surprised at all. I could continue to gush, but I have learned it is best to keep these feelings between us. Suffice it to say, Dave did not ruin my plans, but helped me to pursue God's.

We served in ministry together. I volunteered thirty hours a week at my church, helping women and girls. I couldn't find a job or career in this, so I ended up a bit lost and confused.

That beautiful sunset seemed to be fading. Most people go through this thing called a quarter- life crisis. Mine led us to Massachusetts.

When we moved to New England, it was on the basis that I was a talented student and gifted at teaching. The plan was for me to pursue more schooling so that I could eventually become a teacher. Did I have peace about this? I honestly can't say. We had peace, though, about the move to Massachusetts. That was enough for me.

I dove into classes at seminary, loving every minute of learning. I tried to carve out a path in church history to pursue a PhD, but things just continued to be hard in a way that they never were before. I had unrest and sleepless nights. And then God did something miraculous. Every day for two weeks straight, while I was reading my Bible, I had a vision about a building. I would like to offer something up here for you to consider before you start to grumble about some weird woman having visions. I grew up as a Lutheran, and visions were not something that were talked about or discussed. I really had no idea what this was, nor did I know what to do with it. I wasn't praying for this to happen, and I had no expectation that this would happen.

The building in the vision was a large brick building. On the first floor was a coffee shop. The second floor was filled with work spaces where women could come and work on their GEDs or other groups could happen. The third floor was apartment housing, specifically meant for women who had been sex trafficked.

Every day for two weeks, this was it.

It was a Sunday afternoon at lunch that I told my husband about this. I didn't know what it meant, and he didn't either, but he hugged me and said that we would figure this out together. That night, we were at church where a missionary from Amsterdam was presenting. She talked about what she was doing there and then at the end showed a picture of a huge brick building. She asked us to pray about this building as they were hoping to be given it. They were going to run a coffee shop out of it and have rooms for Bible studies and other groups. They were going to help women who were sex trafficked. And then, she abruptly stopped talking and moved on.

I sat there in tears. I had no idea what God was doing, but I knew I had to find out. After the service, we went and spoke with the missionary. I told her what had been happening, and she began to smile. She said to me that she wondered why she talked about the brick building the way she did. She had felt like God wanted her to say it that way. They were planning to do all of the things she said, but she left out the main purpose for that building, which was to have a Teen Challenge program run out of it. She understood now why she didn't mention that. She looked at me and said, "I don't think God wants you to come to Amsterdam, but I do think He is trying to get your attention."

The next day, I put my plans aside again and began to pray to God about what He wanted me to do. I put the master's program on hold and began to volunteer again. I pursued everything I could and looked to offer as much as possible to women. I did not know how the whole vision was going to happen, but I knew that my dream to become a professor was probably not going to get me there. So I pursued ministry wholeheartedly. Two years later, I was being added on to the pastoral staff as the first female pastor.

Those years were transformative for me. I learned more about compassion and how to love people than at any other time in my life. I was challenged and stretched. I was given opportunities to grow where I had previously been stunted. I was supported as well as critiqued. I grew thick skin, continued to love people, and eventually learned that God was doing something amazing during this time.

Three years after this, as I was seeking to be ordained, this idea of calling came up again. One of the questions you answer when you are seeking to be ordained is how you know that this is what God has called you to do. As I thought more and more about what God had called me to do, I could not shake this vision He had given me. Was I running away from it because it was too scary? While I had worked with women who had been trafficked as a pastor, I really had no idea what to do and couldn't imagine leading an organization that was its sole purpose. But God began tugging at my heart.

There are moments in your life when you simply have to trust God and take the leap. This was one of the moments for me.

Dave and I talked about it, and he too had this amazing

peace about what God was doing. So the next day I spoke with my boss, who gave me his support and as much time as I needed. If you are wondering if you are supposed to be taking a leap in your life, this is a big indication. Do the people who matter most to you support this dream? Do they see the potential in you that you might be blinded to? Are they in your corner giving you the support to take the next steps? If they aren't, you have some serious questions about whether this is the right leap and right time.

I then began to research who was out there to go ahead and get involved. I didn't want to start something; I wanted to become a part of something. I reached out to Amirah and asked if I could chat with them about becoming a volunteer. Little did I know that they were looking to hire an executive director. The chair of the board, Nancy, who I affectionately refer to as a fierce lady, asked to meet with me for coffee, so I agreed.

Halfway through one of the most delightful conversations I have ever had, I realized that this fierce lady was giving me a job interview. The following week, I was meeting with a couple of board members. The third week, I sat down with the entire board. Within a month of taking the leap, I was being asked to become the next executive director for Amirah. Every piece fell into place quite miraculously.

This is a story of God. I have felt ill-equipped at times. I have felt like my sin is too great to be doing anything of worth or value. I have had extreme doubts and depression. I have gone through the gambit of emotions and questions throughout the years. But none of those things matter in the end, because God had a plan all along. I am reminded by Paul that He will use the foolish as well as the wise.[23] So no matter how foolish I feel, He can still do something quite amazing. You may wonder if Amirah has the coffee shop building yet.

As of right now, we don't. But rest assured that this vision has not left my purview.

I got into the work of activism because I took a leap. The reality is that leap started when I was seventeen years old. I've only now begun to realize the beautiful journey He has had me on.

With hope, Stephanie

FOURTEEN

The Disturbing Certainty of Hope

Why do you do this work?
—ACTIVIST

Dear Activist:

I enjoy reading theologians. I have developed a practice of spending a year focusing on one theologian at a time, reading their works and diving in to be refreshed by their lofty thoughts that are far greater than mine.

When I first took this job, I picked up a copy of *Gustavo Gutierrez: Essential Writings.* While he is viewed as a controversial figure in some circles and probably someone I don't fully agree with, I wanted to understand more about liberation theology since I was stepping into a world of liberation. The greatest understanding you can have when reading any theologian is that you will never fully agree with them. The joy is knowing we will never really know how wrong each of us is until we see one another in heaven.

As I read through these various writings, a phrase stuck out that Gutierrez used in describing the belief system of Christianity at its core. He called it "the disturbing certainty of hope."[24] One of the greatest lessons I have learned in my journey with Christ is that when some phrase sticks out to you, it is best to start using it as much as you can. It will transform your life.

At Amirah, we use the hashtag (because every organization needs a hashtag) of #HopeLivesHere. Hope is an integral part of everything we do. Our program director, Heather, says again and again that "hope is a powerful tool for change." You offer hope to someone who has never experienced it, and slowly you watch their lives transform as they believe more and more in themselves and the hope being given to them.

The reality is that this is a disturbing way to live from an outsider's perspective. I am neither a pessimist nor an optimist, but I believe myself to be a realist. Because of my faith, I have decided to coin the term that I am a hope-filled realist.

When I was a kid, we had what was called the flannelgraph at church Sunday school. This was a poster board that had a felt flannel panel glued to it. The teacher would take little paper figures that also had flannel glued to their backs and place them on the board to tell the story. This was transformational storytelling before Bob the Tomato and Larry the Cucumber were in existence.

One of my favorite stories was of Shadrach, Meshach, and Abednego—you know, the three guys from the book of Daniel who would not bow down to the golden image of Nebuchadnezzar. It was a fun story to flannel out as a kid. First there was the *huge* golden image and the three friends standing up while the entire city bowed down. Then the king pointing his finger at the fiery furnace. Then the three men in the fiery furnace with a fourth figure, and finally, magically, the flannel stick figures of the three men all safe and sound with Nebuchadnezzar eating crow. The joys of being a child of the 1980s were limitless.

As I grew older and began to read the story for myself, I was struck with the words of three friends. When threatened with what would be certain death, they replied with full confidence that God was able to deliver them *and would* indeed deliver them. Talk about hope. But then, this realistic statement followed: "But even if he does not, we want you to know, O king, that we will not serve your gods or worship the image of gold you have set up."[25]

Hope-filled realism is at its best right there. It's a bit disturbing, isn't it? Our God can and will deliver us, but even if He decides not to, we still won't cave. Talk about a faith that refuses to be shaken.

Hope and faith are interlinked in such a way that I believe one cannot exist without the other popping into being. As your faith grows in God and who He is, your hope will naturally grow as well. As you see God operate in your life, your hope becomes surer and firmer. It is not some flimsy thing, but it is a strong shield.

That is what I think of as my hope most days—a strong shield deflecting all of the challenges and negativity that would come my way. We face so many challenges every day at Amirah. Working with a population that faces complex trauma is a battlefield of constant negativity. I find the only way I can live my life is to focus and remember who my God is, what He has done, and then the problems seem to melt away as solutions come quite naturally.

In order for this actually to work in your life, you have to be certain in your hope. You need to be prepared for the fact that this certainty will be picked up on by others. I am well aware that if I were to put my hope in human beings, I would not be able to live out this philosophy. As much as I enjoy my time with people, I know they will fail my expectations time and time again. But if I put my expectations on what God can do, even through humans who can fail, this is when I can set my hope on a realistic path where restoration and redemption are key.

We had a woman in our program once who had a rap sheet that would send most people running for the hills. Not only was there a record, but a case was actively open against her while she showed the district attorney she was getting her life together at Amirah. How was a woman with all of that baggage supposed to go out and get a job, which is a part of her vocational trauma recovery?

One of my staff was convinced she would not be able to get hired anywhere, but I smiled and replied to her that I was convinced that this was not an impossible situation; it was a difficult one to be sure, but not impossible.

Within a week, this woman was being hired as a customer service employee at a local business. When they ran the background check and all of these items came to light, they called her into the HR office. She was convinced she was going to be fired, but they talked with her and said that her work was excellent, so they would like to give her a chance. She is now one of their top employees in sales each month, and her open case was closed when she completed the Amirah program. We are working toward her record being expunged as the felonies that she has were a part of her being exploited.

Hope-filled realism leads to opportunities for restoration and redemption. Hope leads to change.

This isn't blind optimism. I don't expect that everything will be easy and filled with rainbows and sunshine. I expect hard work, I expect difficult conversations, I expect that things might work out and that things might not. The answer from God might be no or wait or try a different route. But there is an answer.

My God will save me from the fiery furnace, but even if He doesn't, I still won't cave and worship another. There will be an answer. God is always the answer.

If you ever get the chance to work in any setting where compassion is needed, I beg you here and now to develop in yourself a firm foundation of the disturbing certainty of hope. If you are already in this type of work and are struggling, take some time and dig into who God is. What do you know? What has He shown you? What is He capable of? What does He desire?

When you find those answers, fix your hope on those and nothing else. The challenges will melt away. Because hope is not only a powerful tool for change in those you have a chance to serve, it changes your life as well.

With hope, Stephanie

Notes

1   1 Timothy 4:12 NIV.

2   "Oceans (Where Feet May Fail)," Hillsong United, 2013. This song is often played at youth conventions where youth are praying about their futures.

3   Ephesians 2:10 ESV.

4   Psalm 119:45a ESV.

5   John 1:5, NIV.

6   Psalm 139:12 ESV.

7   Gustavo Gutierrez, *Essential Writings*, 140.

8   1 Kings 19:11–13 ESV.

9   Name changed for protection and privacy.

10   A square is a reference to someone who seemingly has their life together. They probably have a college degree, a solid career, a home or beautiful apartment. They interact well with others and are socially acceptable.

11   Ephesians 3:18 ESV.

12   C. S. Lewis, *The Problem of Pain* (Harper One: New York, 1940), 130.

13   Matthew 14:23; Mark 1:35; 6:46; Luke 6:12 ESV.

14   English Standard Version.

15   1 Thessalonians 5:17 ESV.

16   Line featured in *The Lord of the Rings: The Return of the King* movie, 2003.

17   Psalm 19:1 NIV.

18   John 1:16 ESV.

19   2 Corinthians 4:8–9 ESV.

20   2 Corinthians 4:1, 16 ESV.

21   2 Corinthians 4:15 ESV.

22   C. S. Lewis, *Surprised by Joy*, 223.

23   1 Corinthians 1:27 ESV.

24   Gustavo Gutierrez, *Essential Writings*, 65.

25   Daniel 3:18 NIV.

About the Author

Stephanie Clark is the Executive Director of Amirah. Knowing of the evil of sex trafficking since she was a child, Stephanie has pursued a calling of compassion and liberation for survivors of sexual exploitation. She is a vocal advocate for practical solutions for victims of sexual exploitation, working to provide not only a place for aftercare to exist for these individuals, but develop a greater system of aftercare within our communities. She has a desire to see both global and domestic changes in the view of women.

Amirah has made its mark in the anti-trafficking movement as a leader in aftercare. The whole-person care approach is taught to organizations throughout the region. Stephanie has represented the field of survivor aftercare at the United Nations and is currently spearheading the formation of the coalition of aftercare services. She presented at the Tri-County Human Trafficking Conference in Killington, VT, provided testimony to the Massachusetts State Judiciary Committee, and has been called upon by local leaders within this movement to bring insight for best practices when working with survivors.

She came to Amirah after serving for four years as an Associate Pastor on the North Shore of Boston. Prior to that, she was a small business owner. She has her undergraduate degree in biblical languages from Moody Bible Institute of Chicago.

She comes to New England from Michigan. She and her husband, Dave, enjoy hiking together with their two daughters, Mathia and Nevaeh.

For more information about Amirah or Stephanie, please visit www.amirahinc.org and www.stephaniejoyclark.com.

REFLECTIONS

REFLECTIONS

REFLECTIONS

REFLECTIONS

REFLECTIONS

CPSIA information can be obtained
at www.ICGtesting.com
Printed in the USA
FSHW010520120121
77617FS

9 781973 655572